THE BIBLE
IN ART

THE OLD TESTAMENT

PHAIDON

Frontispiece
MOSES WITH THE TABLES OF THE LAW
Painting by Rembrandt, 1659. *Berlin, Kaiser Friedrich Museum*

THE BIBLE IN ART

MINIATURES·PAINTINGS·DRAWINGS
AND SCULPTURES
INSPIRED BY

THE OLD TESTAMENT

PHAIDON PUBLISHERS INC
DISTRIBUTED BY GARDEN CITY BOOKS
NEW YORK

The translation of Marcel Brion's Introduction is by Lucy Norton.

The Notes have been translated by Elizabeth Osborne

MADE IN GREAT BRITAIN

TEXT AND COLOUR PLATES PRINTED BY HUNT, BARNARD AND CO LTD · AYLESBURY · BUCKS

PHOTOGRAVURE PLATES PRINTED BY VANDYCK PRINTERS LTD · BRISTOL

CONTENTS

INTRODUCTION

'THOU shalt not make to thyself any graven image.' When, at the very dawn of their history, the Children of Israel established it as a law of their religion that no one should make the likeness of any living thing for worship, they took an epoch-making decision, which their leaders and Prophets have expounded century after century. It would be sacrilegious to pretend to give visible form to what is essentially a spirit, to confine the infinite within planes and contours, or to invest with a human or animal face the countenance of the immaterial deity. From this it follows that the cult of images must in itself be perverse and wrong. Since the breath which gave life to the universe has no connection with any substance whatsoever, it is futile to clutter the temples with statues and icons purporting to represent the image of God. As a disembodied spirit, God cannot be adapted to dwell in a body of wood or stone. The all-powerful Creator, who shaped the bodies of the first man and woman from a handful of dust, is so jealous of the prerogative that no man has licence even to imitate His works.

An ancient legend inherited by both Israel and Islam tells how no angel will enter a house where images cast a shadow. The Israelites therefore expressly forbade three-dimensional representations, but even two-dimensional pictures, that cast no shadow unless they are spatially composed with false perspective, were considered equally suspect. The underlying fear of Israel, Islam, the iconoclastic Byzantines, and the Reformation, was that the semblance might become confused with the reality, that the image might be worshipped for itself and not for that which it humbly claimed to represent.

Thus Israel rejected the image in favour of the Word. In their endless journeyings over the face of the earth, and on from earth to heaven, the Children of Israel have elected to travel with no other luggage but the book, the pilgrim's lightest burden. What is more, that Book was not written down until very late in their history. At the beginning it existed only by oral transmission, by virtue of a spoken legend that was both the Word and the Breath of Life. Most ethereal of books, the Scripture was not inscribed on the stones of temples, the walls of pyramids, nor even on papyrus or parchment. It passed from one generation to another, unchanged but ever increasing in riches as the dynasties of kings and priests succeeded one another.

The Book is exclusive and ruthless. Israel, Islam and the Reformation all accepted its commandment that the story it told should never be accompanied by carved or painted illustrations. In any case, such things were unnecessary, for the word-pictures were themselves so vivid and so beautiful that no form of plastic representation could equal their poetic majesty and power. Thus from the very beginning in Israel, the plastic arts, which throve in other contemporary civilizations and were producing masterpieces in Egypt and Mesopotamia, withdrew from competition with the written word. It was from the very fact that they were considered inadequate that images came to be condemned as sacrilegious; for what is unfit to contain the breath of Life, or bear true witness to the Divinity, must not be allowed to exist.

That the Children of Israel sometimes lapsed into the sin of image-carving was probably because men rarely feel sufficiently secure in themselves or their environment to be able to dispense with images through which to ponder and adore the Sublime. The famous story of the Golden Calf is an obvious example of the struggle between the spirit that lives by the Word alone, and the erring flesh that clings to imitations of familiar objects, perhaps because men are lacking in imagination. The simultaneous receiving of the Word by Moses on Mount Sinai, in the midst of a devouring holy fire and, down on the plain, the graven image set up amid dancing and bonfires, is a symbol of eternal significance. Israel feared that the Word might be falsified by the image. They were determined that, when once the Word of Life had been breathed into the original clay, it should be for ever, and that thereafter substance and spirit should remain separate, so that nothing connected with the worship of the One God, the Eternal Spirit, should be contaminated by impure figures of beasts or men. It may well be, indeed, that had Greece not intervened between Israel and the Christianity of the Reformation, the ban on images and icons might never have been lifted. It might have continued to be observed with the same fanatical thoroughness that caused the more orthodox of Moses's followers to massacre the image-carvers after the dramatic overthrowing of the Golden Calf.

It too often goes unnoticed that on that critical day in the history of the Jewish people, when they bloodily affirmed the doctrine of non-representation, another action proclaimed the absolute pre-eminence of the Word. This gesture was that of Moses, when he broke the tablets of stone on which he had written the law which the Lord had dictated. The action was indeed highly significant, for it would be puerile to see nothing but rage and indignation in the movement of the Prophet's hands, as he scattered the pieces of the Holy Stones on which he had scratched the mystic characters, thus freeing the Word from all association with material things. The winds took up the fragments and carried them from nation to nation, from continent to continent. From the spoken word, a primitive people's only means of handing down a tradition, to writing, the final proof of sedentary civilizations that have lost faith in memory, the transition is as drastic as the transition from speech to pictures, especially since the first writings were nothing but pictures, and suggested objects by their visible characteristics.

When the Israelites ceased to depend upon the spoken word and became a writing people, they rejected the ancient forms of script, that were composed of simple pictographs, for example, a man with his hand to his mouth to represent hunger. In their place was substituted a system of abstract characters, such as a man might idly trace in the sand with the end of a stick. These characters were without representational significance; the straight lines and rectangles had no direct connection with ideas and objects and could therefore be accepted as signs for them by a purely abstract convention. They were in no sense intended to be representational, for all representations, however much stylized, even hieroglyphs, are fundamentally picture-writings. For the Scriptures, therefore, representational writing was rejected because it suggested immanence and signs were preferred because they are transcendental. Indeed, if the Scriptures had not been absorbed and adopted by Christianity, they might never have been illustrated in pictures and sculpture. At the very most, there might have been that timid, conscience-stricken concession to the temptation of images which we find in some of the figure-decorations of later Judaism, for example, in the Dura-Europos synagogue, under the influence of the pagan world, the Christian, Roman, Iranian, Egyptian, and Mesopotamian civilizations, whose wealth of images exercised a tantalizing fascination.

According to the original intention, the Jewish Scriptures (the Old Testament, as we now call them) should have remained a Bible without pictures.

Yet no book has ever been so splendidly or so variously illustrated. The great Nordic mythologies were recorded only on the carved sides of the Vikings' ships, on their horse-trappings, ornaments, arms, and clothing, and on their ivory drinking-horns. Homer and the Greek tragedies were not illustrated except on painted vases, or in the frescoes of the Lesche at Delphi. Only the teeming epics of the Ramayana and the Mahabarata that cover the temples of India and the Indian Archipelago can rival in number and magnificence the illustrations to the Holy Writings of Israel; and even in them there is a certain monotony, a want of imagination in the repetitive treatment of the same subjects time after time. Since Christianity first adopted the Old Testament over two thousand years ago, there has never been a book so sublimely and strangely associated with pictures. Today, for perhaps the first time in the history of art (if we except the Reformation, which was a non-aesthetic movement), we are witnessing in the development of abstract art and its successful penetration of religious art, a rebellion by non-representation against the figurative tradition that has lasted for two millenniums.

As Christianity spread across the world, visual illustration of the Holy Scriptures became an important part of the teaching of the Church, for pictures and sculpture have an extraordinary power to educate the mind and stir the emotions. The art of the Bible has benefited by the immense variety of the subjects dealt with, the vast fund of stories, ranging from familiar and picturesque anecdotes to the denunciations of the Prophets, and especially by the wealth of symbolism underlying every allegory. It is a book which all may read, from the ignorant peasant to the most learned scholar. It speaks to each man in the language which he is willing and able to comprehend, in the very words that suit him best, using images that go straight to his heart and understanding. Because it is a religious book, it follows that every event in the history of the Chosen People, or in the lives of the individual characters, is both factual and symbolic. In each happening, the true significance lies in the symbolism, whose meaning is doubly vivid because it attaches to an actual event and not to something purely imaginary. God intended that the experiences of His people should have a universal bearing, and that every man of every period and nation should be able to recognize himself in those whom God elected to be the word-carriers, the representatives of all who came after. Joseph, Tobias, Jacob, David, began by being real people, but their lives took on vastly greater importance when, like the kernel in the stone of the fruit, their actions became charged with the generating power of symbolism.

This is a quality that they share with the great figures of Greek legend and history. Ariadne, Orpheus, Ulysses, Danae, live for us today, and will continue to live as symbolic characters, in the same way that Job, Noah, Samson, or Abraham still exist. As Goethe said, nothing that is perishable can endure eternally unless it is also a symbol. And it is because they were living people as well as symbols that the characters in the Old Testament acquired the miraculous vitality that has been handed down from century to century. First commemorated in the frescoes of the Catacombs and the bas-reliefs on the earliest Christian sarcophagi, their stories have inspired that immense collection of pictures and sculpture to which great artists of every country and period have contributed.

The inspiration is not purely religious, although religion plays an important part in the creation of most works of sacred art. Indeed, the dispute between the innovators and the followers of strict tradition is rather unrealistic. It is sometimes asked, today, whether an artist must necessarily be a believer in order to paint a religious picture, but the very way in which the question is framed shows that there is a confusion of meaning. Must the artist believe in the historical accuracy of a scene when he represents it? Is it not enough that he should recognize its allegorical significance? And surely it is already a great thing that the artist thinks of his work and the act of painting as religious in themselves.

In such an argument, 'believing' should not be used in that sense, although when he paints Old Testament subjects the artist approaches his work in a rather different way from that in which he sets out to paint a 'profane' picture. The Bible is so full of wonders and miracles, so permeated with magic, that nature and the supernatural become fused in perfect harmony. That is why the most realistic artists, the searchers after truth in outward appearances, and the non-realistic, who rarefy the flesh until it is no more than a cloak of light, are both perfectly at home with Old Testament stories of talking beasts, of Angels wrestling with humans and consenting to be thrown, prophetic ghosts or wooden houses that sail over the waters of a great flood and contain all the different varieties of life on earth. The mythology of the Israelites is even stranger than that of their neighbours in Egypt and Mesopotamia. It is the mythology of a nomadic shepherd race, who often saw mirages in the desert, and heard the voice of the one Eternal God in the thunder-clouds that rolled around the fiery mountain-tops. The Children of Israel thought the images of the neighbouring tribes vulgar and materialistic. The animal-headed gods of the Nile Valley, the dragons and chimeras, keeping guard at the gates of Babylonian cities, aroused in them nothing but contempt; for this imaginative people had invented monsters so extraordinary that it was impossible either to describe or represent them.

Like all desert peoples, Israel dwelt in a conception of space and time that was incomprehensible to more sedentary nations of agriculturalists and townsmen. Place and duration had a different meaning for them. Compared with the ordinary temporal and spatial divisions, Israel regarded the desert as a kind of spiritual and geographical constant, attached to a fixed number, for example, the forty years of the Hebrews' flight from Egypt, and the forty days of Christ's temptation in the wilderness. The hills of Tabor, Sinai, Moriah, Golgotha, were to them the High Places, where the forces of earth and heaven, body and spirit, met and wrestled with each other. They were points of combustion, where opposing elements engaged in a life-generating embrace amid the roaring of the thunder and the wind.

The mystery of the spirit that breathed life into inanimate matter seemed to be essentially unrepresentable, and one may understand why Moses laid a curse on image-making. Art historians are now agreed that, at the time when the ban was announced, the peoples of the Near East had not the means to give plastic form to this wholly spiritual conception, even had the fanatical Israelites really desired to reproduce living figures. In this sense the Mosaic reformation, announcing absolute spiritual monotheism, may be said to have been an aesthetic as well as a religious reform. The Golden Calf, whose reign ended with the acceptance of the Tables of the Law, was a symbol of fertility and resurrection among the neighbouring tribes, and among the Jews themselves before their reformation, and it was so regarded by all the Mediterranean peoples. No doubt that it had some connection with the resurrection of the soul as well as the body, but Israel abominated the idea of intermingling soul and body in the same allegory. They well knew the temptation of the sensual forms of religion which dull the brain in a frenzy of excitement, and the danger that lies in seeking for God in the flesh. Men feel the need to adore and to identify themselves with the object of their adoration, and thus flesh and spirit may tend to unite in a way which the Israelites found all the more abhorrent because, at the beginning, they were inclined to fall into the same temptation.

At the opposite extreme from the idea of a desert land scored by the tempests of the infinite, there was the conception of harmonious masses and lines by which gods and men could achieve a perfect and equal harmony. It was a world where, within living memory, the gods had come down to mingle freely with mortals, and had engendered heroes and demigods in the wombs of women. This was the Grecian ideal, and it was elaborated through images because, in Greece, nature itself was a perfect harmony of plastic proportion. Contrary to the Jews, who had turned from the naturalistic representation of figures to the non-representation of the spiritual, the Greeks, in their religious and aesthetic development, tended towards an ever more perfect humanism.

Israel would have failed completely to understand the prayer of Socrates at the end of *Phèdre,* where he says, 'Give me inner beauty and let the outside be in harmony with what lies within.' To the Israelites, the thought that the gods might take on human form and yet lose nothing of their divinity would have seemed sacrilegious and offensive. Part of the Jewish people's objection to Jesus arose from the fact that, like the gods of Greece, He was both God and man, in an indissoluble mingling of their two natures, thus for a long time, the early Christians in Judea disliked representing the human side of the Redeemer.

It might be supposed that the traditional ban on making images would have destroyed any impulse among Christian artists to represent figures, and that they might have continued to evolve an art of allegorical designs, like those in many of the Catacomb paintings and in the mosaics of the palaeo-Christian churches. In the end, however, the Greek conception of harmonious proportion and the union of mind and senses triumphed over the curse laid on the representation of living creatures. It is interesting also to consider to what degree Christian art, at any given moment in its history, or any artist, from Rembrandt, Michelangelo, Mathias Grünewald, Cavallini, Rouault, or Zurbaran, to the Rhenish miniaturists and the Byzantine mosaicists, is composed in varying proportions of Greek sensualism and Jewish spirituality.

13

Where the New Testament is concerned, Christian artists have delighted in recording the scenes of the life of God made man, in realistic natural settings. They represented the various episodes, from the Nativity to the Crucifixion, with the same ease and tender simplicity which the Asian artists applied to the Buddhist *Jakatas* and the life of Krishna. It was a more difficult task to approach the mysteries of the Old Testament, which is so deeply tinged with a rather crude realism and permeated with the archaic mythology of other races. Its stories are often a confused mixture of legend and history, combined with the ever-mysterious symbolism of the East.

Christian art adopted this pictureless Book, whose poetic beauty appealed so strongly to the imagination that visual illustrations seemed redundant. It is important to note that the essentially poetic books, the Psalms, the Song of Songs, and the Books of the Prophets, were the very ones which painters and sculptors avoided, probably because the vividness of the imagery discouraged all attempts to find a plastic equivalent. None the less, and in spite of the apparent difficulties, Christian artists have provided this hitherto unillustrated Testament with a greater wealth of illustration than any other book in existence. It is as though its artistic possibilities had suddenly been freed after two thousand years under, literally, a sentence of death, that had been pronounced because blind fear of images had arisen out of the dread of a revival of idolatry.

What is idolatry? It can take many forms, both crude and subtle, yet it should never be supposed that the artists of Western Christianity claimed to make a likeness of God (the God of Christians as well as Jews), in the reflective Creator with the long white beard, who walked in the Garden and gathered dust to make an image of man, as a worthy habitation for the soul. In the same way, the Greeks were not adoring the statue of a woman when they brought the fine veil that the maidens had woven to the Athena of the Acropolis. Men do not worship material objects for themselves, but for the spiritual power vested in, or represented by, such objects.

The mysteries of the Bible are very different from those in Greek mythology, which are at once more formal and more intimate; they introduce us immediately into a world where we are on level terms with the supernatural. The grand symphonic evolution of Genesis, for example, has a powerful appeal to man's imagination and his love of nature; and the world that emerges little by little from the formless mass of storm-clouds, rain, and mud, is exactly as Hierony-mus Bosch painted it on the outside shutters of the Madrid Triptych. We may see there the writhing forms that try to take shape in the melting-pot of primordial matter. They are indefinite as yet, uncertain whether their develop-ment will be towards rocks or plants. Bosch would seem to have revived some very ancient heresies, for he represents these undecided movements as though the original clay, in its struggle to define itself, retained some elements of independent choice. His dark world developed all the senses one after another, and multiplied itself in an ever-varying profusion of living creatures. Then, as soon as the Breath of Life had animated the molecules of clay and given flesh to what before was purely spiritual, the Earth burst into flower and leaf, ready to welcome the strange menagerie of the mediaeval miniaturists. These were the birds and beasts amid which Man dwelt and reigned when the time came for him to emerge from chaos.

At this moment the history of the human race begins. Greek mythology was not able to tell the story of the beginnings with the simple majesty, or the vividness, of the Old Testament. The allusions in the pre-Socratic writings, to original chaos and the development of species, suggest veiled terror and amazement. Hybrid creatures, many armed, writhe in darkness, unattached legs chase one another, fall in a grotesque embrace, or take to flight, and the broken sentences that tell of such gloomy matings are shrouded in the mystery of 'that stark night with eyes of darkness', which Empedocles describes. 'Thus were born,' he says, 'creatures with feet that twist as they walk, with innumer-able hands, and limbs intertwined. Others are born two-headed, or with four breasts, bulls with human faces, and men with the heads of bulls, others again are androgynous, hybrid creatures with the limbs of women.' The monsters of ancient Mesopotamia and archaic China seem to reappear in these first ancestors of the wisdom and art of Greece, and it is from such as these that Bosch evolved the creatures of his own world of dangerous charm and gloomy sensuality.

The Old Testament, on the other hand, produces living creatures perfectly formed from the moment of their creation. The melting-pot of the elements is immediately transformed into a garden where unicorns, basilisks, and gryphons graze peacefully beside lambs and rabbits, as in the fresco at Ferentillo. More-over, the peace of the Creation would never have been disturbed, nor man's destiny imperilled, had not he himself upset the plan by his own ineluctable doom, which was shared by the entire universe. All the animals and plants, however innocent and peaceful, were involved in the series of catastrophes set in motion by original sin, for the first sin destroyed the harmony of the Creation. A great wind of suffering, disease and death swept through the Garden of Eden, as the Angel with the flaming sword drove Adam out and shut the gate.

All Christian art, perhaps all art whatsoever, is the outcome of that first sin and springs from a longing to recreate the broken harmony and return to the Terrestrial Paradise. From that garden Adam could take nothing except, perhaps, the instinct to hope, the memory of the lost perfection that lies at the root of all artistic creation, the yearning to gather together the scattered fragments and remake the plan of original Creation. Throughout the books of the Old Testament, the entire history of the human race is told in word-pictures. After the Fall comes hard work on the land. Adam becomes a labourer with powerful muscles, as shown in the reliefs of Jacopo della Quercia. Then comes the second Fall, bringing, as its aftermath, the Deluge in which the entire human race is destroyed, save the passengers in that rude Ark tossing on the face of the dark waters. And once again the human adventure begins on virgin soil, for the third time. This is told so concisely and objectively in the Book of Genesis that there is no room for myths and various interpretations of them. More than any other subjects, the Bible stories lend themselves to realistic treatment, and the Italian Baroque artists, led by Caravaggio, discovered there their favourite themes. Between the natural and the supernatural there is a difference of degree, but none of kind, when the subject is one of ordinary everyday reality; for it is an intensity of spiritual power that turns the ordinary into a mystery. Biblical mythology is far less fantastic than the Greek, or at least than that of the Ancient Greeks who, with Geryon, Cerberus, and Typhon, introduced the world of monsters into the crystalline harmony of their perfectly proportioned temples.

The Old Testament writers were not fond of inventing unnatural beasts, and when they mentioned such monsters as Leviathan, they did not describe them; not because they lacked imagination, but because they did not wish to fetter the individual fancy. They preferred to leave it to every man to weave his own conception around that mysterious name, suggestive of such strange and alarming possibilities. Christian artists have had free access to this fund of poetic we hesitate to call them merely symbolic. Like elder brothers they go before us on the paths where Providence has set our feet, protected by the vigilance of Angels, seen or unseen. In such a way, Joseph, abandoned by his family, was guided by prophetic dreams. Moses, Jonah, and Noah were brought safely through the waters, the element endowed with all power and virtue. Tobias searched for the universal remedy that can open the eye of the soul, and at the same time cure physical blindness. Job, on whom God's hand so terribly fell, was overwhelmed with disease and disaster. Isaac was ransomed by the blood of the ram.

All the incidents of this symbolic journey have been recorded in all periods of European art, and at no time has there been a preference for any particular episode. All the stories are chapters of one book, closely linked, inseparable, in the great drama of man's travels through the changes and chances of life. The monsters of the deep, who obeyed Jonah, the lions and the fiery furnace over which Daniel triumphed, are symbolic of the authority that man was granted so that he might rule over the elements. To mark the road of hope that leads the human race from the lost Eden to a new terrestrial paradise, these symbols of divine compassion, forgiveness, and supernatural aid, are set like oases in the desert, so that hope may spring again. In the hour of supreme need, when all earthly help is unavailing, miracles intervene; manna falls from heaven; the rock splits at the point where clear water gushes out of the stone; cured by the image of the serpent, the bites of the real snake are healed.

Does art possess that magic property, so often met with in Israel and, indeed, throughout the whole of the Ancient World, the curative powers of imagery? It would not be the least of the marvels of the Old Testament, wherein miracles are everyday happenings, falling with the suddenness of thunderbolts to strike or exalt. Women characters are sometimes used to lead the men upon their journey and point out the road; heroines like Esther or Judith; unwilling instruments of fate, like Bathsheba, whose lovely body represents both sin and salvation. The Queen of Sheba is the symbol of wisdom, crossing deserts of ignorance and error in the Arabia from whence she came, in order to unite with male wisdom and from this union engender complete perfection. Feminine in her beauty, prophetic in her mystery, the Queen of Sheba is connected with the miracle of the Redemption and the very wood of the True Cross. She is shown in religious painting robed in all the secrecy of the East, accompanied by perfumes and strange music, and heralds on the symbolic plane the procession of the three kings, who took the same road to reach the stable at Bethlehem.

The Procession of the Magi makes us dream of distant lands and sets the imagination brooding on the age-long mystery of the East. But because it belongs to the New Testament, and deals with a humanity more nearly of our own time, it does not appear so strangely exotic as the description of the Queen of Sheba. For here we touch the realm of things which cannot be given plastic expression. The charm of the supernatural suits the poetic version, the great eloquent passages in the Psalm flow out in a wealth of lyrical poetry. 'Deep calleth unto deep at the noise of thy waterspouts, all thy waves and thy billows are gone over me.' The mountains skip like goats, Behemoth plays among the waters of primaeval seas. The imaginative Psalmist finds words to clothe these superhuman truths, but even the genius of Tintoretto and Michelangelo, so masterly in portraying spiritual turmoil, feels here the inadequacy of the plastic form.

Great and various as are the resources of art, there is a limit beyond which they cannot go. They are restricted within the bounds of plastic truth, which can be intensified but less easily expanded. This is because the human figure has continued to be the focal point of European art. Indian and Indonesian sculpture, Chinese painting of the Sung dynasty, the creative genius of the bronze-workers of Shang and Chou, recognized no such limitations or set them at a greater distance. But in Europe, everything that went beyond or above the range of human experience was prudently dismissed as being unpaintable. Only music, for example, Haydn's *Creation*, and Handel's *Messiah*, was capable of competing with the poets. Should artists therefore abandon pictorial methods, properly so-called, and adopt a mode of expression that more nearly approaches poetry and music? The first episodes of the Creation, on the ceiling of the Sistine Chapel, show a Michelangelo who resembles Beethoven as he grapples with great orchestral masses, and lifts, as on the wings of a sublime symphony, movements that have ceased to be purely plastic, according to the ideals of Renaissance art. One of the most characteristic features of the Baroque period was this upsurge of music itself, which was evolving new modern forms of expression, and another was the predominance of musical over plastic qualities in the sculpture and painting of the Counter-Reformation.

The Reformation having revived the Mosaic ban on images, it was only natural that the Counter-Reformation, the most vital trend of Baroque art, should stress the emotional and dramatic content, making its appeal to the senses and drowning reason in a flood of sentiment. The more that Baroque painting and sculpture resembles music, the greater is its charm; indeed, after the beginning of the seventeenth century, there was an important change of position in the arts. No longer were painters and poets the best interpreters of religious feeling; the musicians had surpassed them. With Schütz, Pachelbel, Bach, Vivaldi, Buxtehude, Couperin, Marc-Antoine Charpentier, Lalande, Handel, Haydn, and Mozart, music, in many ways, became a substitute for the plastic arts, and succeeded them as the chief inspirer of religious emotion, a function hitherto magnificently fulfilled by Rembrandt, Giotto, Greco, Tintoretto, Grünewald and Zurbaran. When we listen to the *Jephthah* of Carissimi, we are much nearer to the spirit of the Old Testament than when we look at pictures by Cavallino or Luca Giordano.

It would of course be unfair to be too sweeping in condemning the decline of sacred art since the eighteenth century, for it is always capable of revival in unexpected forms. Non-figurative painting, in particular, may well see the beginning of a totally new kind of religious art. It is possible that the Old Testament stories needed, to make them soul-stirring, the striking simplicity of the mosaics of San Marco at Venice, of the Rhenish miniatures, or of the Franconian and Flemish primitives. Perhaps Tintoretto's visionary *terribilità* suited them best, or the intimate footing on which Rembrandt stood with the Prophets, because he, himself, was also a seer. The splendid evolution that led Christian art from the paintings in the Catacombs to the century of the Great Masters runs parallel with the great adventure of the human race, that, in the Old Testament, begins even before the creation of Man. That spiritual journey, which every man must make in the development of his soul, the sacred books of the image-less people, and the innumerable carved and painted images made to illustrate and explain the different stages, have established an aesthetic tradition two thousand years old, which allows us to hear with extraordinary clarity the authentic sound of the Great Waters in which mankind was born.

Paris, 1956   MARCEL BRION

THE CREATION OF EVE; THE FALL AND THE EXPULSION FROM PARADISE; CAIN AND ABEL.
Enamelled copper dish painted in grisaille by Wenzel Jamnitzer and Pierre Reymond, 1558.
Nuremberg, Germanisches Nationalmuseum (lent by Baron H. Tucher)

THE PLATES

1. THE CREATION. Grisaille painting by Hieronymus Bosch, about 1500. *Madrid, Prado*

2-3. GOD DIVIDES THE LIGHT FROM THE DARKNESS; CREATION OF SUN, MOON AND STARS.
Mosaics, before 1220. *Venice, San Marco*

4. CREATION OF THE FISHES AND THE BIRDS. Mosaic, before 1220. *Venice, San Marco*

5. THE CREATION OF EVE. Mosaic, about 1260. *Florence, Baptistery*

6. GOD CREATES THE SUN, THE MOON, AND THE PLANTS. Ceiling fresco by Michelangelo, 1511. *Vatican, Sistine Chapel*

7. GOD DIVIDES THE WATERS FROM THE EARTH. Ceiling fresco by Michelangelo, 1509-1510. *Vatican, Sistine Chapel*

8. THE CREATION OF ADAM. Ceiling fresco by Michelangelo, 1511. *Vatican, Sistine Chapel*

9. THE CREATION OF EVE. Ceiling fresco by Michelangelo, 1509-1510. *Vatican, Sistine Chapel*

10. THE FALL AND THE EXPULSION FROM PARADISE.
Miniature from Les Très Riches Heures du Duc de Berri, before 1416. *Chantilly, Musée Condé*

11. THE CREATION OF ADAM AND EVE, THE FALL AND THE EXPULSION FROM PARADISE.
Bronze relief by Ghiberti, about 1436. *Florence, Baptistery*

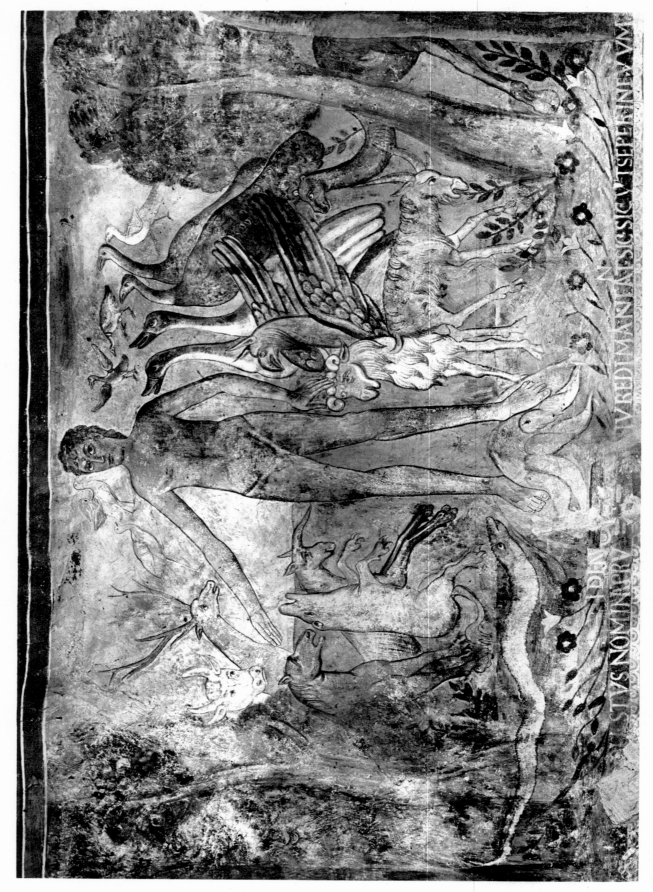

12. ADAM NAMING THE BEASTS. Fresco, 12th century. *Ferentillo, S.Pietro*

13. THE CREATION OF THE BIRDS, BEASTS AND FISHES. English miniature, 14th century. *London, British Museum*

14. THE FALL. Painting by Hugo van der Goes, about 1470. *Vienna, Kunsthistorisches Museum*

15. THE EXPULSION OF ADAM AND EVE FROM PARADISE.
Fresco by Masaccio, about 1427. *Florence, S.Maria del Carmine*

16. ADAM AND EVE LABOURING. Stone relief by Wiligelmo, about 1115. *Modena, Cathedral*

17. ADAM AND EVE TOILING. Stone relief by Jacopo della Quercia, about 1430. *Bologna, S.Petronio*

18. THE SACRIFICE OF CAIN AND ABEL. Bronze relief, about 1010. *Hildesheim, Cathedral*

19. CAIN AND ABEL. Bronze relief by Bartolomeo Bellano, about 1484-1490. *Padua, S.Antonio*

20. THE STORY OF CAIN AND ABEL. Bronze relief by Ghiberti, about 1436. *Florence, Baptistery*

Côme nie seig comenda a noel faire vne arche et y mettre vne paire de toutbestes pour le deluge.   Côme noel apis le deluge anua a terre et mist hors le bestail et fist sacrifice et planta la vigne.

21-22. NOAH AND THE ARK. French miniatures, 1423. *London, British Museum*

23. THE FLOOD. Intarsia after a design by Lorenzo Lotto, about 1524-1530. *Bergamo, S. Maria Maggiore*

24. THE FLOOD. Mosaic, before 1220. *Venice, San Marco*

25. THE FLOOD. Ceiling fresco by Michelangelo, about 1509. *Vatican, Sistine Chapel*

26. THE FLOOD. Painting by Nicolas Poussin, 1664. *Paris, Louvre*

27. THE SACRIFICE OF NOAH. Painting by Bernardo Cavallino, about 1650. *Samuel H. Kress Collection. Houston, Museum of Fine Arts*

28. THE DRUNKENNESS OF NOAH. Ceiling fresco by Michelangelo, about 1509. *Vatican, Sistine Chapel*

29. THE STORY OF NOAH AFTER THE FLOOD. Bronze relief by Ghiberti, about 1440. *Florence, Baptistery*

30. THE DRUNKENNESS OF NOAH. Stone relief by Jacopo della Quercia, about 1430. *Bologna, S.Petronio*

Comit on edihia la tour de babiloine. et le languege fust mue en. lx xij Languegues. et les anges la despeviient.

31. THE TOWER OF BABEL. French miniature, 1423. *London, British Museum*

32. THE TOWER OF BABEL. Mosaic, about 1220. *Venice, San Marco*

33. THE TOWER OF BABEL. Detail of a Flemish miniature from the
Breviarium Grimani, about 1500. *Venice, Biblioteca Marciana*

34. THE TOWER OF BABEL. Painting by a follower of Hubert van Eyck,
first half of the 15th century. *The Hague, Mauritshuis*

35. THE TOWER OF BABEL. Painting by Pieter Bruegel, 1563. *Vienna, Kunsthistorisches Museum*

36. LOT AND HIS DAUGHTERS. Painting attributed to Dürer, about 1498.
Samuel H. Kress Collection, Washington, National Gallery of Art

LOT AND HIS DAUGHTERS. Painting by Lucas van Leyden, about 1521. *Paris, Louvre*

37. LOT'S DEPARTURE. Pen and ink drawing by Rembrandt, about 1660. *London, British Museum*

38. LOT FLEEING FROM SODOM. Painting by Rubens, 1625. *Paris, Louvre*

39. ABRAHAM ENTERTAINING THE ANGELS. Etching by Rembrandt, 1656

40. THE DISMISSAL OF HAGAR. Engraving by Lucas van Leyden, about 1508

41. SARAH COMPLAINING OF HAGAR TO ABRAHAM. Pen and ink drawing by Rembrandt, about 1640. *Paris, Louvre*

42. THE DISMISSAL OF HAGAR. Painting by Rembrandt, 1640. *London, Victoria and Albert Museum*

43. **THE DISMISSAL OF HAGAR.** Painting by Jan Steen, about 1660. *Dresden, Gemäldegalerie*

44. HAGAR AND THE ANGEL AT THE FOUNTAIN. Painting by Ferdinand Bol, about 1665. *Amsterdam, Rijksmuseum*

45. ABRAHAM'S SACRIFICE. Marble statue by Donatello, 1421. *Florence, Museo di S.Maria del Fiore*

46. ABRAHAM'S SACRIFICE. Statue, about 1230. *Chartres, Cathedral*

47. ABRAHAM'S SACRIFICE. Etching by Rembrandt, 1655

48. ABRAHAM'S SACRIFICE. Painting by Rembrandt, 1635. *Leningrad, Hermitage*

49. REBEKAH AND ELIEZER AT THE WELL; REBEKAH WATERING ELIEZER'S CAMELS.
French miniature, about 1356. *Paris, Bibliothèque Nationale*

50. REBEKAH WATERING ELIEZER'S CAMELS; THE JOURNEY OF REBEKAH AND ELIEZER.
Mosaic, before 1200. *Monreale, Cathedral*

51. REBEKAH DRAWING WATER FOR ELIEZER AND HIS CAMELS. Miniature from the Vienna Genesis, middle of the 6th century. *Vienna, Staatsbibliothek*

REBEKAH RECEIVING JEWELS; REBEKAH TELLING OF HER ENCOUNTER. Miniature from the Vienna Genesis, middle of the 6th century. *Vienna, Staatsbibliothek*

53. REBEKAH AND ELIEZER. Painting by Nicolas Poussin, 1648. *Paris, Louvre*

54. REBEKAH AND ELIEZER. Painting by Murillo, about 1668. *Madrid, Prado*

56. ISAAC BLESSING JACOB. Painting by Murillo, about 1670. *Leningrad, Hermitage*

57. JACOB'S DREAM. Painting by Domenico Feti, about 1616. *Vienna, Kunsthistorisches Museum*

JACOB WRESTLING WITH THE ANGEL. Painting by Rembrandt, about 1659. *Berlin, Kaiser Friedrich Museum*

58. JACOB TENDING LABAN'S FLOCKS. Painting by Ribera, about 1639. *Madrid, Museo Cerralbo*

59. JACOB'S DREAM. Painting by Ribera, about 1639. *Madrid, Prado*

60. JACOB'S DREAM. Painting by Murillo, about 1670. *Leningrad, Hermitage*

61. JACOB'S DREAM. Ceiling fresco by Raphael and Baldassare Peruzzi, about 1512-1514. *Vatican, Stanza d'Eliodoro*

62. RECONCILIATION OF JACOB AND ESAU. Painting by Rubens, about 1625-1627. *Munich, Alte Pinakothek*

63. JOSEPH TELLING HIS DREAM. Grisaille painting by Rembrandt, before 1638. *Amsterdam, Rijksmuseum*

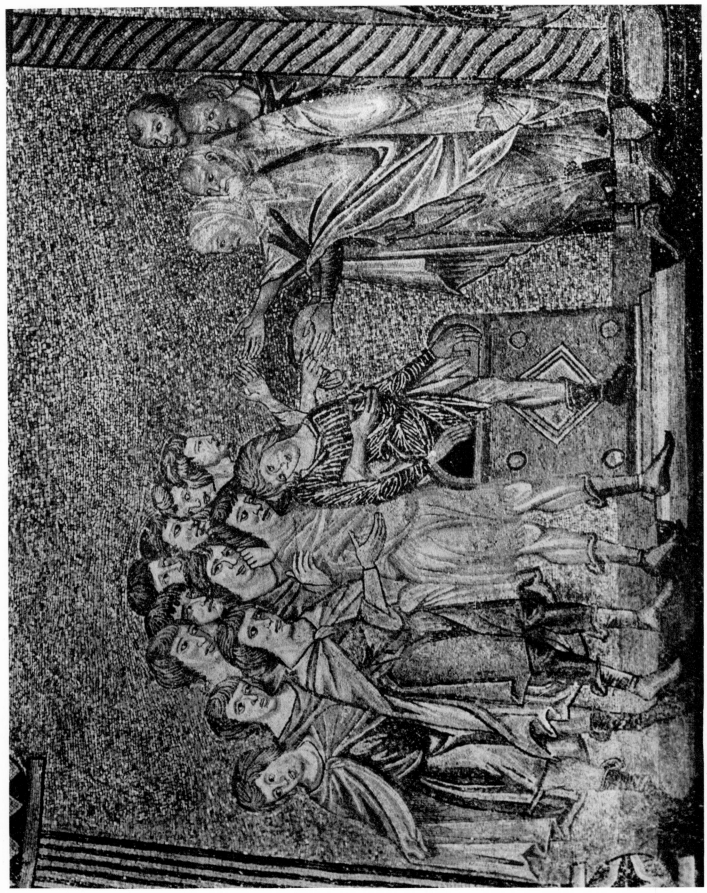

64. JOSEPH LIFTED FROM THE PIT AND SOLD TO THE ISHMAELITES. Mosaic, before 1300. *Florence, Baptistery*

65. JOSEPH JOURNEYS TO EGYPT WITH THE MIDIANITES. Mosaic, before 1300. *Florence, Baptistery*

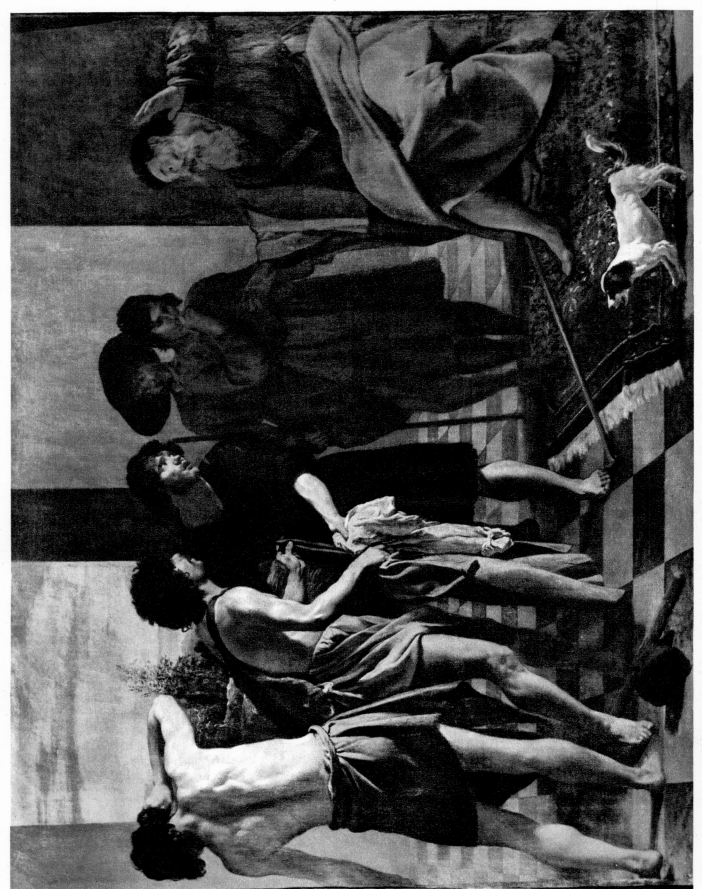

66. JACOB RECEIVING THE BLOODSTAINED COAT OF JOSEPH. Painting by Velazquez, about 1630. *Madrid, Escorial*

68. JOSEPH AND POTIPHAR'S WIFE. English miniature, about 1200. *Munich, Staatsbibliothek*

69. POTIPHAR'S WIFE ACCUSING JOSEPH. Miniature from the Vienna Genesis, middle of the 6th century.
Vienna, Staatsbibliothek

70-71. JOSEPH SOLD TO POTIPHAR; JOSEPH CAST INTO PRISON. Mosaics, before 1300. *Florence, Baptistery*

72. THE STORY OF JOSEPH IN EGYPT. Bronze relief by Ghiberti, about 1440. *Florence, Baptistery*

73-74. JOSEPH DISTRIBUTING CORN IN EGYPT; THE MEETING OF JACOB AND JOSEPH.
Ivory reliefs, middle of the 6th century. *Ravenna, Cathedral*

75. JACOB LETS BENJAMIN DEPART WITH THE BRETHREN, Painting by Barent Fabritius, about 1655.
The Hague, Mauritshuis

76. THE SILVER CUP FOUND IN BENJAMIN'S SACK; JOSEPH REVEALS HIMSELF TO HIS BRETHREN.
Detail of Plate 72.

77. POTIPHAR'S WIFE ACCUSING JOSEPH. Detail of a painting by Rembrandt, 1655. *Leningrad, Hermitage*

78. JACOB BLESSING EPHRAIM AND MANASSEH. Painting by Rembrandt, 1656. *Cassel, Museum*

79. BENJAMIN'S JOURNEY INTO EGYPT
English miniature, about 1200. *Munich, Staatsbibliothek*

80. JACOB'S JOURNEY INTO EGYPT. Miniature from the
Admont Bible, about 1130-1150. *Vienna, Staatsbibliothek*

81. THE MEETING OF JACOB AND JOSEPH AT GOSHEN. Mosaic, before 1300. *Florence, Baptistery*

82. JOSEPH RECEIVES HIS BRETHREN UNRECOGNISED AND IS MOVED TO TEARS.
Miniature from the Vienna Genesis, middle of the 6th century. *Vienna, Staatsbibliothek*

83. THE BURIAL OF JACOB. Detail of a miniature from the Ashburnham Pentateuch, 7th century.
Paris, Bibliothèque Nationale

84-86. THE STORY OF JOSEPH:
JOSEPH SENT TO HIS BRETHREN AND SOLD BY THEM TO THE ISHMAELITES; JOSEPH IN EGYPT AND
JOSEPH'S MEETING WITH JACOB; JACOB BLESSING EPHRAIM AND MANASSEH; THE DEATH OF JACOB.
Ivory reliefs 12th century. 84 and 85 in *Berlin, Kaiser Friedrich Museum*. 86 in *London, British Museum*

87-89. THE FINDING OF MOSES; MOSES SLAYING THE EGYPTIAN; MOSES TAKEN INTO THE
HOUSE OF JETHRO. Ivory reliefs, about 310-320. Lipsanoteca in *Brescia, Museo Civico Cristiano*

90. THE FINDING OF MOSES. Painting by Giambattista Tiepolo, about 1755-1760. *Edinburgh, National Gallery of Scotland*

91. THE FINDING OF MOSES. Painting by Sebastien Bourdon, about 1650. *Samuel H. Kress Collection, Washington, National Gallery of Art*

92. THE FINDING OF MOSES. Painting by Paolo Veronese, about 1565. *Madrid, Prado*

Coment moyses met sa coroune sur la teste moyses. e il le prent e gette v sou: e il le comaunde mettre a mort. a syre sire autresi uoluntiers il maungereit vn charboun ardaunt.

Coment moyses t
 oue le payen: e aire le Juyf.

93. AN EPISODE FROM THE YOUTH OF MOSES; MOSES SLAYING THE EGYPTIAN.
Miniature from the Queen Mary Psalter, about 1310. *London, British Museum*

94. MOSES TENDING JETHRO'S SHEEP; THE ANGEL OF THE LORD BEFORE THE
BURNING BUSH; MOSES RECEIVING THE TABLES OF THE LAW.
Relief, about 430. On the wooden door of *S. Sabina, Rome*

95. MOSES BEFORE THE BURNING BUSH. Detail of a fresco by Botticelli, about 1482. *Vatican, Sistine Chapel*

MOSES BEFORE THE BURNING BUSH. Painting by Domenico Feti, before 1614. *Vienna, Kunsthistorisches Museum*

96. GOD APPEARING TO MOSES IN THE BURNING BUSH. Ceiling fresco by Raphael and Baldassare Peruzzi, about 1511-1514. *Vatican, Stanza d'Eliodoro*

97. THE SLAYING OF THE FIRST-BORN. Fresco by Bernardino Luini, about 1522. *Milan, Brera*

98. THE CHILDREN OF ISRAEL PREPARE TO LEAVE EGYPT. Fresco by Bernardino Luini, about 1522. *Milan, Brera*

99. THE DESTRUCTION OF PHARAOH'S HOST. Fresco by Bernardino Luini, about 1522. *Milan, Brera*

100. THE DELIVERANCE OF THE ISRAELITES. Fresco by Bernardino Luini, about 1522. *Milan, Brera*

101. SCENES FROM THE YOUTH OF MOSES. Fresco by Botticelli, 1482. *Vatican, Sistine Chapel*

102. MOSES AND HIS FAMILY RETURNING TO EGYPT. Fresco by Pinturicchio, 1481-1483. *Vatican, Sistine Chapel*

103. THE CROSSING OF THE RED SEA. Fresco by Cosimo Rosselli, 1481-1483. *Vatican, Sistine Chapel*

104. THE CROSSING OF THE RED SEA. Painting by Lucas Cranach, 1530. *Munich, Alte Pinakothek*

105. THE GATHERING OF THE MANNA. Painting by Tintoretto, about 1591-1594. *Venice, S. Giorgio Maggiore*

106. THE GATHERING OF THE MANNA. Painting by Nicolas Poussin, 1639. *Paris, Louvre*

107. THE GATHERING OF THE MANNA. Painting by Bacchiacca, about 1540. *Samuel H. Kress Collection, Washington, National Gallery of Art*

108. THE GATHERING OF THE MANNA. Painting by Dirk Bouts, about 1464-1468
Louvain, St. Pierre

109. MOSES STRIKING WATER FROM THE ROCK. Fresco, 4th century. *Rome, Catacomb of S. Callisto*

110. MOSES STRIKING WATER FROM THE ROCK. Fresco, School of Raphael, about 1519. *Vatican, Loggie*

1. MOSES STRIKING WATER FROM THE ROCK. Painting by Tintoretto, about 1577. *Venice, Ceiling of the Scuola di San Rocco*

112. MOSES RECEIVING AND PROCLAIMING THE LAW. Carolingian miniature from the Grandval Bible, about 840. *London, British Museum*

MOSES. Detail of a fresco, 4th century. *Rome, Catacomb of S. Callisto*

113. MOSES RECEIVING THE LAW. Limestone relief, 7th century. *Berlin, Kaiser Friedrich Museum*

114. MOSES RECEIVING THE LAW. Detail of a bronze relief by Ghiberti, about 1436. *Florence, Baptistery*

115. MOSES WITH THE TABLES OF THE LAW; THE WORSHIP OF THE GOLDEN CALF. Fresco by Cosimo Rosselli, 1481-1483. *Vatican, Sistine Chapel*

116. THE CHILDREN OF ISRAEL IN THE WILDERNESS. Fresco, School of Raphael, about 1519. *Vatican, Loggie*

117. MOSES. Detail of a painting by Jan Gossaert, about 1520.
Vienna, Kunsthistorisches Museum

118. MOSES. Marble statue by Michelangelo, about 1513-1516. *Rome, S.Pietro in Vincoli*

119. THE COVENANT ON MOUNT SINAI. Miniature from the Ashburnham Pentateuch, 7th century. *Paris, Bibliothèque Natie*

120. MOSES ON MOUNT SINAI. Miniature from the Sarajevo Haggadah, 14th century. *Sarajevo, Museum*

121. WORSHIP OF THE GOLDEN CALF. Miniature from the Admont Bible, about 1130-1150. *Vienna, Staatsbibliothek*

122. THE MESSENGERS FROM CANAAN. German miniature, about 1260-1270. *Munich, Staatsbibliothek.*

123. THE DESTRUCTION OF KORAH. Miniature by Fouquet, about 1475. *Paris, Bibliothèque Nationale*

124. THE DESTRUCTION OF KORAH. Detail of a fresco by Botticelli, 1482. *Vatican, Sistine Chapel*

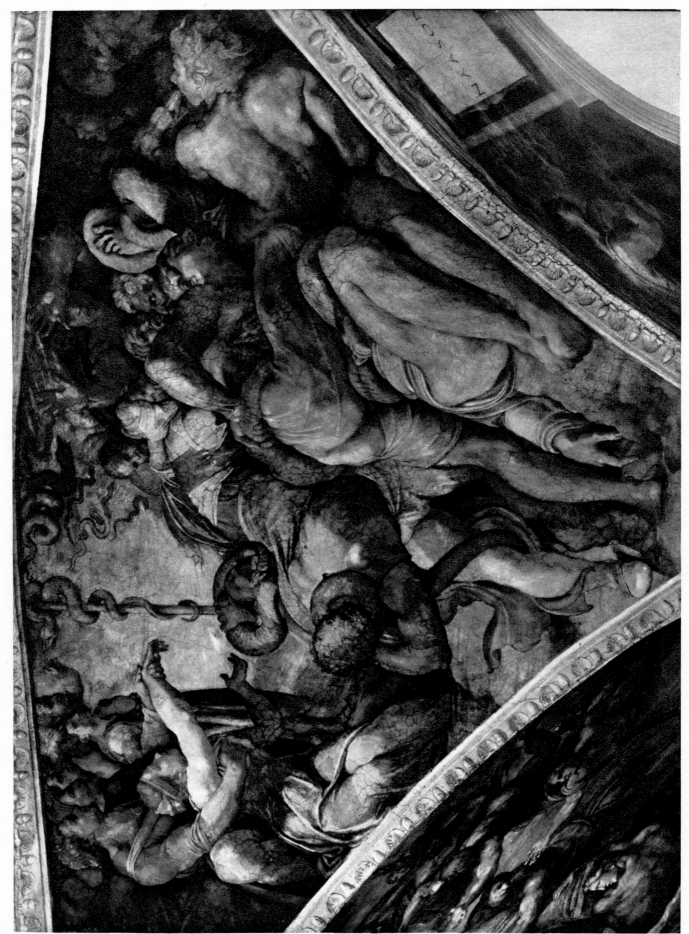

125. THE BRAZEN SERPENT. Ceiling fresco by Michelangelo, 1511. *Vatican, Sistine Chapel*

126. THE BRAZEN SERPENT. Painting by Rubens, about 1635-1638. *London, National Gallery*

127. MOSES, AARON AND HUR.
Miniature from a Hebrew Pentateuch, before 1300. *London, British Museum*

128. MOSES, AARON AND HUR. Detail of a mosaic, about 432-440. *Rome, S.Maria Maggiore*

129. MOSES BLESSING THE PEOPLE. Miniature from the Sarajevo Haggadah, 14th century. *Sarajevo, Museum*

130. BALAAM AND THE ASS. German miniature, 1457. *Munich, Staatsbibliothek*

131-132. GOD SPEAKS TO BALAAM; BALAAM AND THE ANGEL. French miniatures, about 1250. *Oxford, Bodleian Library*

133. MOSES BEING SHOWN THE PROMISED LAND. Detail of a fresco by Signorelli, about 1481-1483.
Vatican, Sistine Chapel

134. MOSES RECEIVING THE LAW. Detail of a fresco by Cosimo Rosselli, about 1481-1483. *Vatican, Sistine Chapel*

135. THE CHILDREN OF ISRAEL MOURNING OVER MOSES. Detail of a fresco by Signorelli, about 1481-1483.
Vatican, Sistine Chapel

136. THE STORY OF JOSHUA. Bronze relief by Ghiberti, about 1440. *Florence, Baptistery*

137. THE FALL OF JERICHO. Miniature by Fouquet, about 1475. *Paris, Bibliothèque Nationale*

138-140. THE FALL OF JERICHO; ACHAN'S TRESPASS AND PUNISHMENT; JOSHUA'S VICTORY.
Sections from the Joshua Scroll, 10th century. *Vatican, Library*

141. THE SIEGE OF JERICHO. Mosaic, about 432-440. *Rome, S.Maria Maggiore*

vo dem ftreit chom . ꝛ

⹋ ꝓ epte den ftreit alſo ge
wunnen hett vnd von
dem ftreit hin wid'cha
⸫⸫ hett er ain tocht'als

142. JEPHTHAH MEETING HIS DAUGHTER.
German miniature, 1457. *Munich, Staatsbibliothek*

143. JAEL AND SISERA. Pen and ink drawing after the Ma
of Flémalle, about 1430. *Brunswick, Herzog Anton Ulrich Mus*

144. JAEL AND SISERA. English miniature from the Queen Mary Psalter, about 1310. *London, British Museum*

145-146. DEBORAH RIDING INTO BATTLE WITH BARAK; SAMSON SETTING THE FIELDS ON FIRE
French miniatures, 1252-1270. *Paris, Bibliothèque Nationale*

147. SAMSON SLAYING THE PHILISTINES WITH AN ASS'S JAWBONE. Floor mosaic by Paolo di Martino, 1426
Siena, Cathedral

148. MANOAH'S SACRIFICE. Painting by Rembrandt, 1641. *Dresden, Gemäldegalerie*

149. SAMSON'S WEDDING. Painting by Rembrandt, 1638. *Dresden, Gemäldegalerie*

150. SAMSON THREATENING HIS FATHER-IN-LAW. Painting by Rembrandt, 1635. *Berlin, Kaiser Friedrich Museum*

151. SAMSON WRESTLING WITH THE LION. Painting by Rubens, about 1625. *Stockholm, National Museum*

SAMSON AND DELILAH. Painting by Van Dyck, before 1620. *London, Dulwich Gallery*

152. SAMSON AND DELILAH. Painting by Francesco Morone, about 1510. *Milan, Museo Poldi Pezzoli*

153. RUTH FINDING FAVOUR WITH BOAZ. French miniature, 1317.
Paris, Bibliothèque Nationale

154. RUTH AND BOAZ. Miniature from the Admont Bible, about 1130-1150. *Vienna, Staatsbibliothek*

155. RUTH AND BOAZ WITH THE REAPERS. French Miniature, about 1250. *New York, Pierpont Morgan Library*

156. DAVID TENDING THE SHEEP; DAVID ANOINTED BY SAMUEL
Miniature from the Winchester Psalter, about 1150-1160. *London, British Museum*

157. DAVID ANOINTED BY SAMUEL. Byzantine miniature, 10th century. *Paris, Bibliothèque Nationale*

158. DAVID AND GOLIATH. Bronze relief by Ghiberti, about 1440. *Florence, Baptistery*

159. DAVID ANOINTED BY SAMUEL. Silver dish from Cyprus, 7th century.
New York, Metropolitan Museum

160. DAVID AND GOLIATH. Intarsia after a design by Lorenzo Lotto, about 1524-1530. *Bergamo, S. Maria Maggiore*

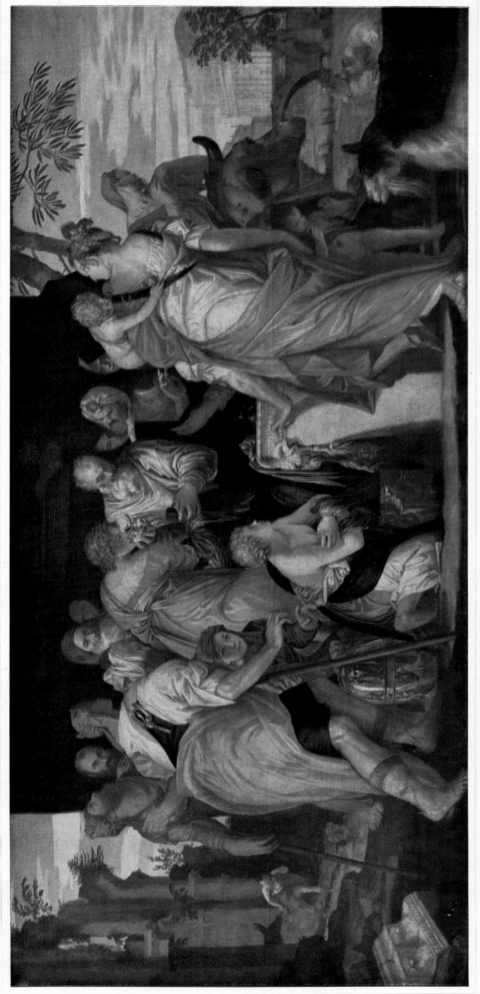

THE ANOINTING OF DAVID. Painting by Paolo Veronese, about 1554. *Vienna, Kunsthistorisches Museum*

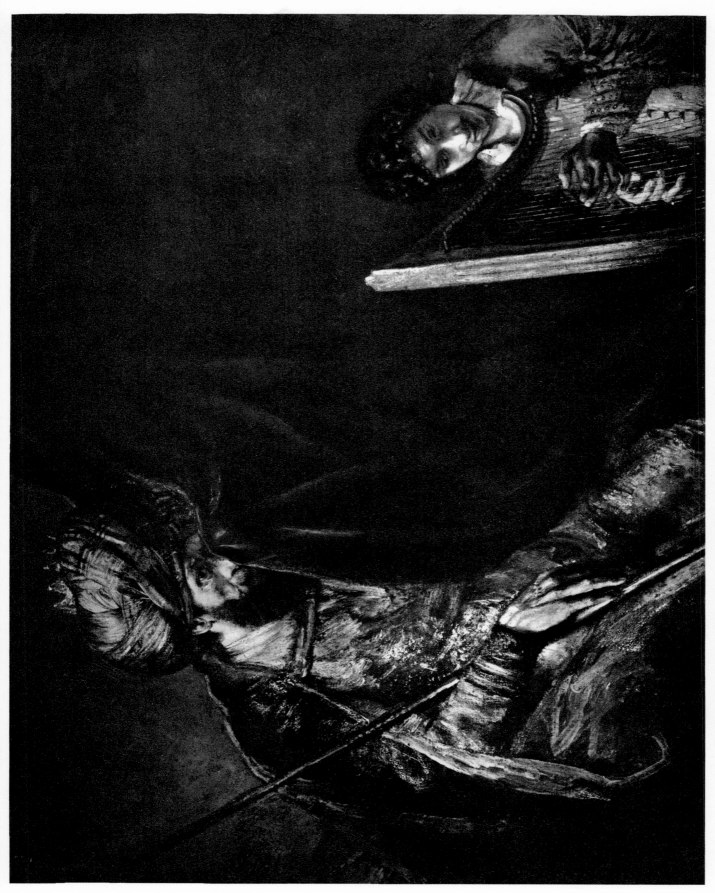

161. DAVID PLAYING THE HARP BEFORE SAUL. Painting by Rembrandt, about 1657. *The Hague, Mauritshuis*

162. DAVID PLAYING THE HARP BEFORE SAUL. Engraving by Lucas van Leyden, about 1509.

163. SAUL AND THE WITCH OF ENDOR. Painting by Salvatore Rosa, about 1660-1670. *Paris, Louvre*

164. DAVID. Bronze statue by Donatello, about 1430-1432. *Florence, Museo Nazionale*

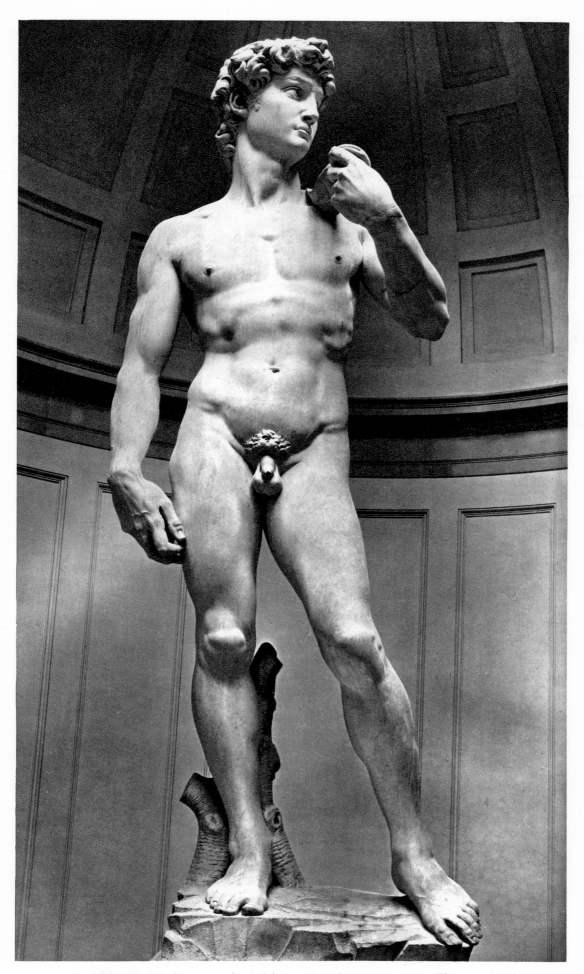

165. DAVID. Marble statue by Michelangelo, about 1501-1504. *Florence, Accademia*

166. DAVID WITH THE HEAD OF GOLIATH. Painting by Caravaggio, about 1605-1606. *Rome, Galleria Borghese*

57. DAVID WITH THE HEAD OF GOLIATH. Painting by Girolamo Forabosco, about 1665. *Vaduz, Liechtenstein Gallery*

168. THE DEATH OF SAUL AND HIS SONS. Miniature from the Lambeth Bible, about 1150. *London, Lambeth Palace*

DAVID PLAYING THE HARP. Byzantine miniature, 10th century. *Paris, Bibliothèque Nationale*

9. DAVID MOURNS FOR SAUL AND JONATHAN. Miniature by Fouquet, about 1475. *Paris, Bibliothèque Nationale*

170. THE RECONCILIATION OF DAVID AND ABSALOM. Painting by Rembrandt, 1642. *Leningrad, Hermitage*

71. KING DAVID. Detail of a statue by Claus Sluter, about 1400. *Dijon, Moses Fountain of the Chartreuse de Champmol*

172. DAVID THE PSALMIST. English miniature from the Rutland Psalter, about 1250. *Belvoir Castle*

173. ABSALOM CAUGHT IN THE TREE. French miniature, about 1250. *Toledo, Cathedral Library*

174. DAVID AND NATHAN; DAVID'S PENANCE. Byzantine miniature, 10th century. *Paris, Bibliothèque Nationale*

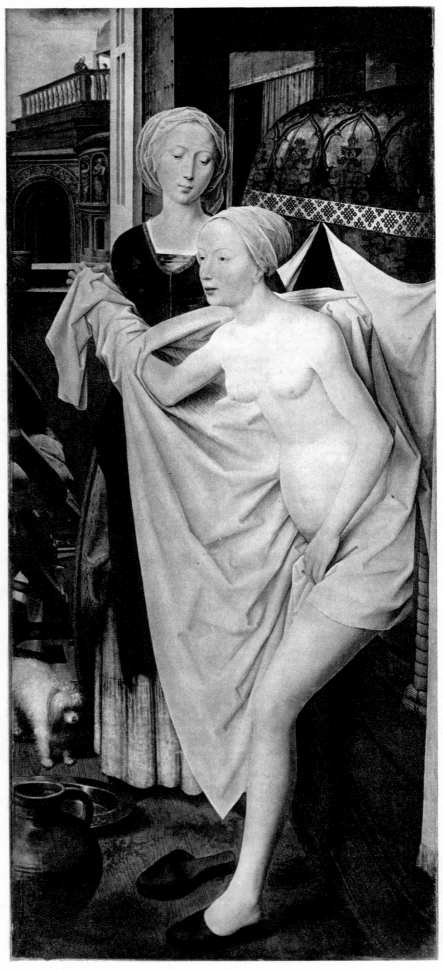

175. BATHSHEBA AT HER TOILET. Painting by Memling, about 1485.
Stuttgart, Staatsgalerie

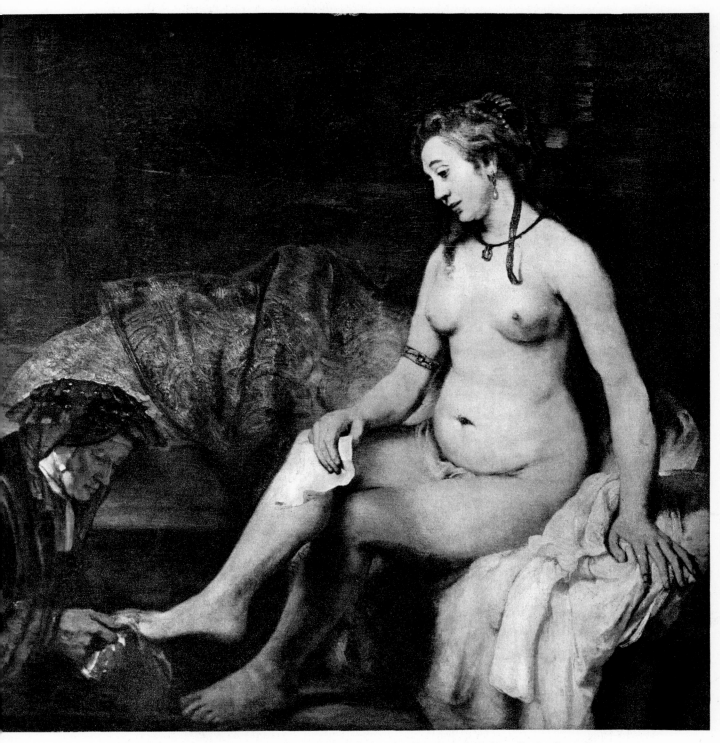

176. BATHSHEBA AT HER TOILET. Painting by Rembrandt, 1654. *Paris, Louvre*

177. THE JUDGEMENT OF SOLOMON. Detail of a painting by Giorgione, about 1508. *Kingston Lacey, Bankes Collection*

178. THE JUDGEMENT OF SOLOMON. Painting by Rubens, about 1615-1617. *Copenhagen, State Museum*

179. THE JUDGEMENT OF SOLOMON. Ceiling fresco by Raphael, about 1509-1511. *Vatican, Stanza della Segnatura*

8. THE EMBARKATION OF THE QUEEN OF SHEBA. Painting by Claude Lorrain 1648. London National Gallery

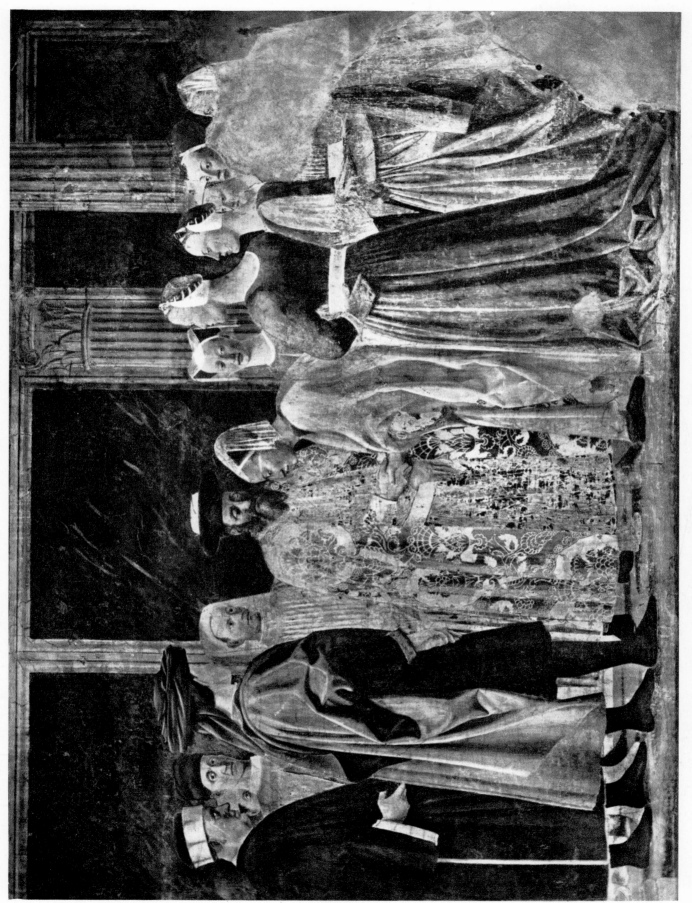

181. SOLOMON AND THE QUEEN OF SHEBA. Fresco by Piero della Francesca, about 1452-1459. *Arezzo, S. Francesco*

182. SOLOMON AND THE QUEEN OF SHEBA. Bronze relief by Ghiberti, about 1440. *Florence, Baptistery*

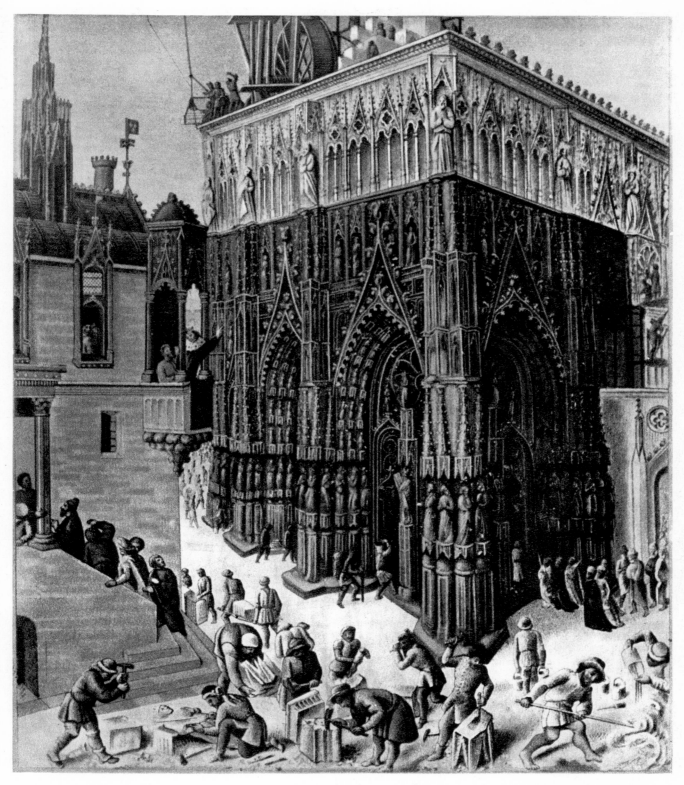

183. THE TEMPLE OF SOLOMON. Miniature by Fouquet, about 1475. *Paris, Bibliothèque Nationale*

184. THE DEFEAT OF SENNACHERIB. Painting by Rubens, about 1616. Munich. Alte Pinakothek

185. KING REHOBOAM. Fragment of a fresco by Holbein, about 1525. *Basle, Öffentliche Kunstsammlung*

186. ISAIAH. Fresco by Raphael, about 1512. *Rome, Sant'Agostino*

ISAIAH. Ceiling fresco by Michelangelo, 1509. *Vatican, Sistine Chapel*

187. JEREMIAH. Ceiling fresco by Michelangelo, about 1511. *Vatican, Sistine Chapel*

189. ELIISHA AND THE WOMAN FROM SHUNAM. Painting by Gerbrandt van den Eeckhout, 1664. *Budapest, Museum*

190. THE CALLING OF JEREMIAH. Miniature from the Winchester Bible, about 1140.
Winchester Cathedral

191. ISAIAH. Relief, about 1140. *Souillac, Abbey Church*

192. JEREMIAH. Statue by Claus Sluter, about 1400. *Diion, Moses Fountain of the Chartreuse de Champmol*

193. ISAIAH. Statue by Claus Sluter, about 1400. *Dijon, Moses Fountain of the Chartreuse de Champmol*

194. MICAH. Detail from the Ghent Altar by Jan van Eyck, 1432. *Ghent, St. Bavo*

195. ZECHARIAH. Statue by Claus Sluter, about 1400. *Dijon, Moses Fountain of the Chartreuse de Champmol*

196. THE ASCENSION OF ELIJAH. Relief, about 430. On the wooden door of *S. Sabina, Rome*

197. JOB PLAGUED BY THE DEVIL. Stone relief, about 1230. *Chartres, North Portal of the Cathedral*

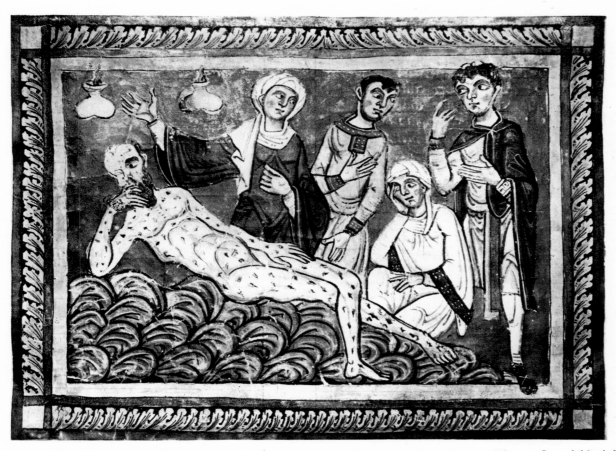

198. THE MOCKING OF JOB. Miniature from the Admont Bible, about 1130-1150. *Vienna, Staatsbibliothek*

199. JOB AND HIS WIFE. Painting by Dürer, about 1503-1504. *Frankfurt, Städelsches Kunstinstitut*

200. JOB AND HIS FRIENDS. Painting by Luca Giordano, about 1695. *Madrid, Escorial*

201. THE DESTRUCTION OF THE CHILDREN OF JOB. Painting by Bernaert van Orley, 1521. *Brussels, Museum*

202. THE STORY OF JOB. Painting by the Master of the Legend of St. Barbara, about 1480-1483. *Cologne, Wallraf-Richartz Museum*

203. THE STORY OF JONAH. Sarcophagus, second half of the 3rd century. *Rome, Lateran Museum*

204-205. JONAH AND THE WHALE. Ivory relief, about 310-320. Lipsanoteca in *Brescia, Museo Civico Cristiano*

206.-208. DANIEL IN THE LIONS' DEN; SUSANNA AND THE ELDERS; SUSANNA BEFORE DANIEL.
Ivory reliefs, about 310-320. Lipsanoteca in *Brescia, Museo Civico Cristiano*

210. DANIEL IN THE LIONS' DEN. Painting by Rubens, about 1616. Formerly in the *Collection of the Duke of Hamilton*

211. THE THREE YOUTHS IN THE FIERY FURNACE. Fresco, about 230-240. *Rome, Catacomb of S.Priscilla*

212. SUSANNA AND THE ELDERS. Fresco, second half of the 4th century. *Rome, Catacomb of S.Pietro and Marcellino*

213. THE HEALING OF TOBIT. English drawing, about 1200-1225. *Cambridge, University Library*

214. THE ARCHANGEL RAPHAEL DEPARTING FROM TOBIT AND HIS FAMILY.
Painting by Rembrandt, 1637. *Paris, Louvre*

215. TOBIT AND HIS WIFE. Painting by Rembrandt, 1659. *Rotterdam, Collection of W. van der Vorm Sr.*

216. TOBIAS AND THE ANGEL. Painting by Adam Elsheimer, about 1600-1610. *London, National Gallery*

217. TOBIAS AND THE ANGEL. Painting by Girolamo Savoldo, about 1540. *Rome, Galleria Borghese*

TOBIAS AND THE THREE ARCHANGELS. Painting by Botticini, about 1467. *Florence, Uffizi*

218. JUDITH WITH THE HEAD OF HOLOFERNES. Painting by Botticelli, about 1490. *Amsterdam, Rijksmuseum*

219. JUDITH WITH THE HEAD OF HOLOFERNES. Painting by Artemisia Gentileschi, about 1621-1626.
Florence, Palazzo Pitti

220. JUDITH WITH THE HEAD OF HOLOFERNES. Painting by Rubens, about 1616-1618.
Brunswick, Herzog Anton Ulrich Museum

221. ESTHER BEFORE AHASUERUS. Detail of a Cassone painting by Filippino Lippi, about 1478. *Chantilly, Musée Con*

22. MORDECAI LAMENTING BEFORE THE GATES OF THE PALACE. Cassone painting by Botticelli, about 1478.
Rome, Pallavicini Collection

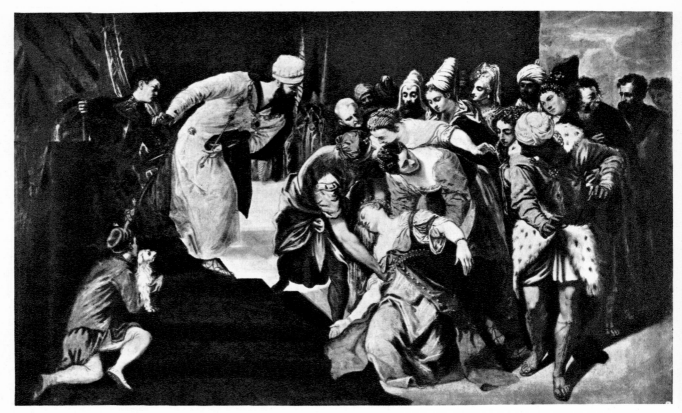

223. ESTHER SWOONING BEFORE AHASUERUS. Painting by Tintoretto, about 1545. *Madrid, Escorial*

224. THE WRATH OF KING AHASUERUS. Painting by Jan Steen, about 1660. *Birmingham, Barber Institute*

225. HAMAN IN DISGRACE. Painting by Rembrandt, about 1660. *Leningrad, Hermitage*

226. THE TABLES OF THE LAW.
Detail of a painting by Joos van Ghent, about 1475. *Urbino, Palazzo Ducale*

NOTES ON THE PLATES

ACKNOWLEDGEMENTS

We wish to express our gratitude to all Museums and Collections who have provided us with photographs and accorded us their permission to reproduce their works.

In particular we should like to thank the Bankes Collection in Kingston Lacey; the British Museum, the Governors of the Dulwich College Picture Gallery, the National Gallery in London; the Bodleian Library in Oxford; the Metropolitan Museum, the Pierpont Morgan Library and the Samuel H. Kress Collection in New York; the Rijksmuseum in Amsterdam; the Kaiser Friedrich Museum in Berlin; the Städelsches Kunstinstitut in Frankfurt; the Mauritshuis in The Hague; the Bayerische Staatsbibliothek and the Alte Pinakothek in Munich; the Germanisches National Museum in Nürnberg; the Convento di Priscilla and the Biblioteca Apostolica Vaticana in Rome; the National Museum in Stockholm; the Staatsgalerie in Stuttgart; the Kunsthistorisches Museum and Osterreichische Staatsbibliothek in Vienna.

Photographs were also obtained from the Courtauld Institute, the Warburg Institute, Country Life, Archives Photographiques in Paris, Archives Centrales Iconographiques in Brussels, and Messrs. Alinari in Florence, Anderson in Rome, Brogi in Florence, Foto Mas in Madrid, Foto Paoletti in Milan, and Foto Villani in Bologna.

THE following notes intend to give, besides the usual information about the artist, technique and date, a short description of each picture; they do not, however, aim at an iconographical or typological analysis. This would require much more space and lies outside the scope of this book. The aim was to establish the link between each picture and the corresponding passage in the Bible, so that *both can be read together*, thus helping to understand the picture's content, and to facilitate the identification of the figures; occasionally, too, to point out some significant detail in the background, in the subsidiary figures and in the setting, always with regard to the rendering of the Bible text.

To explore the bigger theological and historical issues which are involved, has not been attempted.

London, 1956   HEIDI HEIMANN

NOTES ON THE PLATES

1. THE CREATION OF THE WORLD. Genesis I. 1–13. Grisaille painting by Hieronymus Bosch in the Prado, Madrid. About 1500.

The closed wings of the triptych 'The Garden of Earthly Delights' or 'The Millennium' as it has been called in a recent special study (Wilhelm Fränger, The Millennium of Hieronymus Bosch, 1952). The wings when opened, show on the left 'The Garden of Eden' and on the right 'Hell'. However the main picture is interpreted, the subject of the outside panels is clear, though very individually shaped: the world, just created by the Word, is suspended, floating in the dark outer universe. The tiny figure of God is seated in the top left corner. His words of creation are written above: IPSE DIXIT ET FACTA SUNT IPSE MANDAVIT ET CREATA SUNT. Within the globe is shown, foreshortened, the disc of the world; on it are the first rocks, hills, caves, plants. The whole is wrapped in mist, overshadowed by clouds and rain: the primeval landscape. Fränger is certainly right in pointing out that this unique picture owes something to the alchemist's retort as well as to the symbolic crystal globe which in mediaeval paintings the Almighty often holds in His hands.

2–4. Details from a mosaic in the southernmost cupola of the narthex of San Marco in Venice. Second decade of the 13th century. The whole mosaic shows in three rows and twenty-four scenes the creation from the very beginning to the Expulsion and the Labours of Adam and Eve. The Venetian mosaicist followed a very old Alexandrian tradition, such as we find preserved for instance in the Cotton Bible. Each day is hailed and symbolized by an angel, so that on the seventh Day seven angels are standing round the Creator.

2. CREATION OF LIGHT AND DARKNESS. The First Day, Genesis I. 1–5. Light and Darkness are represented as two discs from which rays issue. The angel of the first day stands behind Light, his arms raised in a gesture of acclamation.

3. CREATION OF SUN, MOON AND THE STARS. The Fourth Day. Genesis I. 14–19. The sphere of the world, covered with a pattern of stars with the sun shining from above and the crescent moon below, rolls along on clouds between God and four Angels who symbolize the Fourth Day.

4. CREATION OF THE FISHES AND BIRDS. The Fifth Day. Genesis I. 20–23. The creatures are clearly distinguished. Amongst the birds are an owl, a duck, a swan, a raven; among the fish a crab and a sea-monster.

5. CREATION OF EVE. Genesis II. 21–25. Mosaic on the Dome of the Baptistery San Giovanni in Florence. Second half of the 13th century.

The third in a set of Genesis pictures, starting with God creating the world and finishing with the Flood. The scene follows the Bible text in an established mediaeval pattern. Adam is asleep on a little slope; Eve is just emerging with her hands raised in adoration towards God who is enthroned on a sphere with a scroll in His left hand and blessing with His right. The Garden of Eden is indicated by the trees filling the background and by the four rivers 'out of Eden' (Genesis II. 11–14) which emerge as four oddly shaped rivulets from the slope on which Adam rests.

6–9. Four Frescoes from the Sistine Ceiling by Michelangelo at the Vatican, Rome. The Story of the Genesis is shown in nine central panels closely related structurally and iconographically to the surrounding scenes and figures, as admirable in each of its details as in the relation of each part to the others and to the whole. Begun in 1508, the entire ceiling was finished in 1512.

6. GOD CREATES THE SUN AND MOON: HE CREATES THE VEGETATION. The Third and Fourth Days. Genesis I, 11–19. The second fresco on the ceiling of the Sistine Chapel, about 1511.

God, with young spirits crouching under His cloak, makes a commanding gesture, creating the sun in the centre and the moon to the right. On the left, rushing towards the back, God is seen again, and with one hand raised He commands the plants to rise.

7. GOD DIVIDES THE WATERS FROM THE EARTH. The Second Day. Genesis I. 6–8. The third fresco on the ceiling of the Sistine Chapel. About 1509–1510.

Probably inspired too by the second verse of Genesis '. . . and the spirit of God moved upon the face of the waters.' God is looking down on the beginning of creation with spirits enclosed in His shell-like cloak.

8. CREATION OF ADAM. The Sixth Day. Genesis I. 26–27, II. 7. The fourth fresco on the ceiling of the Sistine Chapel, 1511.

God is again surrounded by spirits which crowd under His cloak. He stretches out His hand and without touching Adam's hand, He infuses a soul into the inanimate body.

9. CREATION OF EVE. Genesis II. 21–22. 1509–1510.
This is the central panel of the whole ceiling. Eve emerges
from behind Adam, who lies in heavy slumber, her arms
raised in adoration.

10. THE GARDEN OF EDEN; THE TEMPTA-
TION, THE FALL AND EXPULSION. Genesis
III. Miniature, fol. 25 recto, from Les Très Riches Heures
du Duc de Berry by Pol de Limbourg and his brothers,
Chantilly, Musée Condé. Before 1416.
This Book of Hours is famous for its most exquisite
illustrations which are equally outstanding in execution
and in inventiveness. This full page illumination shows
four scenes in one landscape: The Temptation, the Fall,
God reproving Adam and Eve, the Expulsion. The
arrangement is still mediaeval in form but the figure of
the kneeling Adam to whom Eve offers the apple,
derives – like other features of the Limbourgs – from
Italian sources and is Renaissance in feeling. An elaborate
Gothic fountain stands in the middle of the Garden of
Eden; outside the low encircling wall lies the yet un-
tilled earth in bare little hills.

11. CREATION OF ADAM AND EVE, FALL
AND EXPULSION. Genesis II. Bronze Relief from
the third door of the Baptistery in Florence by Lorenzo
Ghiberti. About 1436.
The so-called Porta del Paradiso shows in ten panels
episodes from the Old Testament beginning with the
Creation of Adam and Eve and finishing with King
Solomon and the Queen of Sheba. Ghiberti achieves by
different means a very similar composition to that of Pol
de Limbourg. His circular space is not enclosed by a wall
but formed by the figures of the sleeping Adam, God and
the Angels looking down. In the centre of the circle Eve
rises, supported by four putti. The Fall happens outside
this magic circle on the left, under the shade of several
large trees, and in the foreground is the Creation of Adam.
To the right the Angel chases Adam and Eve through the
gate out into the world, commanded by God who
appears with a host of Angels above. A comparison of
these two works of art, so near in time and composition,
is most revealing.

12. ADAM NAMING THE BEASTS. Genesis
II. 19. Fresco in S. Pietro near Ferentillo (Badia). 12th
century.
A scene not often represented in the series of the Creation,
but it is by no means unique. It is the third in a set of Old
Testament pictures. The composition clearly stems from a
Byzantine prototype, whereas the animals and birds
show a new realism. Amongst the animals there is a
unicorn; the pig appears to be just receiving its name.
Among the birds there is a griffon.

13. CREATION OF BIRDS AND BEASTS.
Genesis I. 20–25. Miniature, fol. 2 verso in the so-called

Holkham Bible (formerly Holkham Hall, Ms. 666, now
British Museum, Add. 47682). English, early 14th
century.
God sits full face with His right hand raised and His left
pointing downward. The birds include peacock, owl,
parrot, hawk, eagle, swallow, duck, magpie, goldfinch,
rook, swan, heron, etc.
The beasts are on the left: lion, lioness, elephant, camel,
horse, unicorn; on the right: ape, bear, two dogs, bull,
ram, goat, stag, boar, hare. The text in Anglo-French
says that God created all things by a word, and nothing,
except man and woman, with His hands.

14. THE FALL. Genesis III. 1–7. Painting by Hugo van
der Goes, Vienna, Kunsthistorisches Museum. About
1470.
A single picture, not belonging to any cycle, which in
itself is quite a novel and significant fact. Up to the 15th
century this scene was always one in a series of The Creation, whatever the technique: book illumination, mosaic,
fresco. But from then onwards an incident like The Fall
could be isolated and made the subject of a separate
picture. The serpent, as often, is represented as a kind of
'monster', half human, half animal, in this case with a
woman's head on a salamander's body. The scene is
set in an open, hilly landscape without visible enclosure
of the 'Garden'. Eve has just tasted one apple and plucks
another for Adam. An iris plant grows between them.

15. THE EXPULSION OF ADAM AND EVE
FROM THE GARDEN OF EDEN. Genesis III.
23–24. Fresco by Masaccio in the Brancacci Chapel in
S. Maria del Carmine, Florence. About 1427.
The narrow panel – top left at the entrance to the chapel –
is most effectively used. The gate is just visible on the
left; otherwise the space is entirely filled by the desolate
pair of Adam and Eve driven out by the Angel with a
sword, pointing forward away from Eden.

16. ADAM AND EVE LABOURING. Genesis
III. 19 and 23. Stone relief by Wiligelmo on the façade of
the cathedral at Modena. First quarter of the 12th
century.
This is a relief belonging to a frieze of the Genesis stories
which runs horizontally along the façade of the cathedral.
Traditionally different tasks are allotted to Adam than to
Eve. Wiligelmo, however – one of the few sculptors
known by name in the 12th century – shows them as
perfect partners. Eve, as strong as her mate, is tilling the
ground using the same instrument, an adze, bending over
with the same stooping movement as he does.

17. ADAM AND EVE TOILING. Genesis III. 19 and
23. Stone relief by Jacopo della Quercia on the jambs of
the Porta Maggiore at S. Petronio in Bologna. About
1430.

The reliefs by Quercia run vertically parallel with the door; there are five on each side starting at the top. This one is the fifth, the lowest, on the left. The heavy garments which completely enveloped the figures by Wiligelmo have given way to free floating cloaks which leave most of the bodies uncovered. Adam is using a spade; Eve, confronting him upright, is spinning, while her two sons, Cain and Abel, are playing at her feet.

18. SACRIFICE OF CAIN AND ABEL. Genesis IV. 3–5. Bronze relief from the Bernward door made for St. Michael at Hildesheim; since 1130 in the cathedral of Hildesheim. Between 1008–1015.
The door shows sixteen reliefs: the eight on the left are scenes from the Old Testament, starting with the Creation of Adam and Eve finishing with the slaying of Cain, confronting eight scenes from the New Testament. Artistically and technically an astonishing achievement, the door was commissioned, inspired and made for S. Bernward, Bishop of Hildesheim. – Abel presents a lamb, Cain a sheaf of corn. God's hand, large in an enormous halo of flames, is turned towards Abel. Some rudimentary plants grow on the strip of ground and sprout from the corners.

19. CAIN AND ABEL. Genesis IV. 3–8. Bronze relief by Bartolomeo Bellano in the S. Antonio, Padua. About 1484–90.
One of twelve bronze reliefs with scenes from the Old Testament that decorate the choir-screen on the inside. Hilly landscape, with Abel's flock in the foreground dotted about at irregular intervals; on opposite slopes the two altars, Abel's on the left, whose flames flare up in a blaze towards heaven, and on the right Cain's – he has thrown himself down before his altar – on which the sacrifice has not been taken up. Between the two a cleft and there in the foreground, in the very centre of the panel, the crime itself. Cain straddles the prostrate Abel and is aiming the deadly blow with his club.

20. CAIN AND ABEL. Genesis IV. 2–16. Bronze relief from the third door of the Baptistery in Florence by Lorenzo Ghiberti, about 1436 (see No. 11).
The whole story of Cain and Abel is told in full on this *one* panel: from their childhood with Adam and Eve (left hand upper corner), to Abel 'a keeper of sheep' with his dog watching his flock in the middle ground, to Cain 'a tiller of the ground' with his yoke of two oxen ploughing right in front, to their sacrifice (right hand upper corner) on top of a mountain with God blessing Abel's offering, to the slaying with a raised stick, and finally to the cursing of Cain. The whole seems effortless contained in one frame without overcrowding, so great is the skill of the artist in devising appropriate scenery and in reducing the scale of the figures towards the background.

21–22. MINIATURES by the Bedford Master, so-called after the Book of Hours in the British Museum, Add. 18850, which was executed for the Duke of Bedford on the occasion of his marriage to Anne, sister of Duke Philippe of Burgundy, in 1423, by a French book illuminator.

21. BUILDING THE ARK. Genesis VI. 14–16. British Museum, Ms. Add. 18850, Fol. 15 verso.
A full page illumination illustrates in rich and technically interesting detail the construction of the Ark – one man in the foreground is using a drill, others are cutting the timber, tools are lying about. Noah standing near the Ark is pointing upwards giving orders. Behind the big frame of the Ark lies an as yet peaceful landscape: ships are sailing, a shepherd is tending his flock but some animals are already starting for the Ark.

22. EXIT FROM THE ARK AND THE STORY OF NOAH. Genesis VIII. 18–22; IX. 22–23. British Museum, Ms. Add. 18850, Fol. 16 verso.
Like the above a full page illustration: The Ark is now grounded with a gangway up: on it beasts are just walking to the shore, in front a bear followed by a stork. A peacock, a lion and some cattle are already on firm ground. To the right, Noah has built his altar which the hand of God from the clouds is blessing. In the receding waters houses re-appear and corpses are carried away. In the foreground Noah is tending his vineyard. Under a shed two of his sons are busy with the vine harvest, while Noah lies drunk in front and is discovered by Ham.

23. THE FLOOD. Genesis VII. 1–12. Intarsia after a design by Lorenzo Lotto made by Gian Francesco Capodiferro, his son Zanino and his brother Pietro for the choir stalls at Santa Maria Maggiore in Bergamo. Between 1524–1530.
Lotto has chosen the beginning of the Flood; the animals are entering the Ark. Noah is seen on his knees from the back as if imploring the Almighty to stay His hand. On lower ground to the left drowned men and beasts are already swirled away by the onrushing waters.

24. NOAH AND THE GREAT FLOOD. Genesis VII. 23–24; VIII. 6–20; IX. 8–19. Mosaics on the barrel-vault between two cupolas in the narthex of San Marco, Venice. First half of the 13th century.
The six scenes on this vault have to be read from the top left corner, where the disaster of the Flood, 'every living substance was destroyed', is illustrated: men and beasts are drowned and rain is pouring down like a curtain. To the right is the Ark with Noah sending out the dove which in the row below is returning to him. Next Noah, releasing the beasts, has come out of the Ark, followed by

his three sons with their wives. The sign of the covenant, the rainbow, frames this group. Noah is seen for the fourth time in the lowest row to the left of an altar, sacrificing. To the right, on a rocky piece of land are the animals, just released, amongst them a couple of leopards, foxes, hares and a lion are jumping about.

25. THE FLOOD. Genesis VII. Detail from the Fresco by Michelangelo on the ceiling of the Sistine Chapel (see No. 6–9). About 1509.
The flood is the eighth, i.e. the last but one, in the sequence of Michelangelo's frescoes on the Genesis. In actual fact, he started painting from this end, so that in chronological order this is the second one executed. The ark is afloat towards the back. Men are struggling frantically to gain a foothold on its platform and are trying to get inside with the help of a ladder. In the foreground others have found temporary refuge in a tub-like boat in which they fight bitterly to keep it from being overloaded by fresh arrivals. The desperate struggle for survival in the face of the onrushing waters has never before been depicted with such horrible intensity.

26. THE FLOOD. Genesis VII. Painting by Nicolas Poussin in the Louvre, Paris. 1664.
As opposed to Michelangelo, who shows humanity in despair, Poussin paints the elements in distress. His picture is one of four in which he uses four scenes from the Old Testament to illustrate the four Seasons. Spring: The Garden of Eden; Summer: Ruth and Boaz among the Reapers in the field; Autumn: The Messengers from Canaan (The Promised Land); and Winter: The Deluge. Only a few humans remain to be seen. Water is everywhere; a boat is capsizing in the swiftest part of the current; another in the right foreground, is filling up with the last survivors. A streak of lightning cleaves the sombre rain clouds. Houses, of which only the roofs remain visible, are silhouetted against its light. And in the left foreground massive and lowering, there crouches a huge serpent on a crag still above water, symbol of sin and corruption.

27. THE SACRIFICE OF NOAH. Genesis VIII. 20–22. Painting by Bernardo Cavallino. About 1650. Samuel H. Kress Collection. Houston, Museum of Fine Arts.
The family of Noah, now delivered, are assembled around a carved altar. A lamb lies on the altar-table as a thank-offering, and Noah himself kneels behind it, his eyes raised to heaven in adoration. To his left stand the womenfolk, his three daughters-in-law, and his own wife; on his right the sons, gazing upwards.

28. THE DRUNKENNESS OF NOAH. Genesis IX. 20–23. Fresco by Michelangelo on the ceiling of the

Sistine Chapel, Vatican. About 1509 (see Nos. 6–9, 25). This is the ninth and last in the series of Genesis panels in the Sistine Chapel. Noah, old and weary, a jug and a bowl next to his couch, lies under a wooden hut in front of a barrel, sleeping heavily. His three sons are standing to the right pointing with outstretched arms; one, the nearest, is just about to cover the father with a cloak. On the left in the background Noah is seen once more tilling the barren earth with a spade.

29. THE STORY OF NOAH AFTER THE FLOOD. Genesis VIII. 18–22; IX. 1–22. Bronze relief by Lorenzo Ghiberti from the third door of the Baptistery San Giovanni in Florence; about 1440 (see Nos. 11, 20).
In the middle background a group of eight people: Noah with his wife and his three sons with their wives have just left the Ark. Animals are already walking about; a stag and an elephant to the left, a pair of lions and some cattle on the right. God in a circle of Angels is blessing Noah's sacrifice. And on the left under an arbour, round which vine is growing, Noah lies drunk; his three sons, two with averted eyes, are standing next to him.

30. THE DRUNKENNESS OF NOAH. Genesis IX. 21–23. Stone relief by Jacopo della Quercia on the jambs of the Porta Maggiore at S. Petronio in Bologna. About 1425–38 (see No. 17).
This is the fourth relief to the right of the door. The locality is conveyed by the vine forming an arbour. The confined space is taken up completely by the figures. Noah lies, another Adam, unconscious on the ground, discovered in his 'nakedness' by his sons, one of whom is just dropping a cloak over him. Behind the trunk of the vine a young woman is hiding, a very rare occurrence in this scene.

31. THE TOWER OF BABEL. Genesis XI. 3–9. French. Full-page illumination from the Book of Hours of the Duke of Bedford. British Museum, Add. 18850. fol. 17 v. 1423. (See Nos. 21–22.)
The tower in process of construction is both imaginary and contemporary. The technical equipment is shown in just as much detail as in the building of the Ark (see No. 21) from the same manuscript. Contrary to the injunction in the Bible '. . . let us make brick, and burn them thoroughly', obviously a stone building is being erected; appropriately enough lime is being mixed under a lean-to on the left, while a block-and-tackle is at work on the right. Near the top of the tower two wooden platforms have been put up, from which the men build higher and higher. But at that point two angels are descending upon them, one with a sword, the other with an axe; several of them draw back, one has already fallen to the ground.

THE TOWER OF BABEL. Woodcut by Hans Holbein.
Before 1526.

32. THE TOWER OF BABEL. Genesis XI. 3–9.
Mosaic on the barrel-vault in the narthex of San Marco,
Venice. About 1220. (See Nos. 2–4.)
The erection and destruction are here shown separately.
On the left is the tower in the course of construction;
wooden ramps and scaffolding enable the labourers to
hoist the bricks and mortar. God attended by three angels
surveys the scene of activity from a cloud. On the right,
the same building, but bereft of all building tackle; the
Lord has 'come down' (Gen. XI. 7) surrounded by a host
of angels, to reduce the evil enterprise to nothing. He
stands on a kind of socle directly above the door, and four
groups of people, gesticulating to indicate 'that the Lord
did there confound the language of all the Earth', are
leaving the building, to 'scatter them abroad'.

33. THE TOWER OF BABEL. Genesis XI. 3–9.
Detail of a full-page Flemish illumination from the
Breviarium Grimani in the Biblioteca Marciana, Venice
(fol. 206 recto). About 1500.
The gigantic proportions of this tower, already well on
the way to completion, can be gauged by the fact that
the ramp leading around the tower and up to its top is
wide enough to take a horse and cart. Many details of
technical interest: on the left, part of the quarry from
which the stone for the building is taken.

34. THE TOWER OF BABEL. Genesis XI. 3–4.
Panel painting, recently attributed to the circle of Hubert
van Eyck, in the Mauritshuis, The Hague. First half of the
15th century.
This representation is unusual in that the actual building
of the tower has only just begun. It has not yet reached
beyond the first storey, but the gigantic proportions are
already evident from the contrasted small figures of the
builders. Unusual are also the location of the tower by
the sea-shore, and the rounded windows. The Orient is
indicated by a camel in the foreground.

35. THE TOWER OF BABEL. Genesis XI. 3–4.
Painting by Pieter Bruegel in the Kunsthistorisches
Museum, Vienna. Signed and dated 1563.
Bruegel depicts wantonness before it is punished by God;
a huge building stretches upwards, more like a fortress or
citadel than a tower, and strangely reminiscent of the
Colosseum in Rome. The immense height of the building
is most forcibly demonstrated by the diminutive size of
the human beings. The Colossus reaches up to the clouds.

36. LOT AND HIS DAUGHTERS. Genesis XIX.
22–26. Reverse of a painting: Madonna and child, by
Dürer, in the Samuel H. Kress Collection, Washington,
National Gallery of Art. About 1498.
This unusual picture was first attributed to Dürer by
Max J. Friedländer in 1934. This attribution has been
accepted by E. Buchner and H. Tietze. The coat of arms
of two Nuremberg patrician families are to be seen in the
painting.
Lot – his fur-lined coat doubling back as he walks –
strides forward, his water-bottle on his staff, followed by
his daughters; one carries a distaff, thread and a casket, the
other balances a bundle on her head. On the road, a long
way back, the dark silhouette of the mother petrified into
salt; still further back, Sodom and Gomorrah, over which
fire and brimstone are raging.

37. LOT'S DEPARTURE. Genesis XIX. 15–23. Pen
and wash drawing by Rembrandt in the British Museum,
London. About 1660.
In this, one of the last drawings by Rembrandt for the
story of Lot, he illustrates verse 16: 'And while he
lingered the men laid hold upon his hand and upon the
hand of his wife and upon the hand of his two daughters,
the Lord being merciful unto him and they brought him
forth, and set him without the city.' Lot, in distress,
hesitates between the two angels, who direct him to walk
towards the left, followed by the two daughters, all set
for the journey, the furthest one with a bundle on her
head. The wife, barely recognizable, is sketched in
between Lot and the Angel.

38. LOT FLEEING FROM SODOM. Genesis XIX.
15–16. Painting by P. P. Rubens. Louvre, Paris. Dated
1625.
Rubens has chosen the same moment in the story of Lot
as Rembrandt in his drawing, but this being a finished
picture, he presents the incident in great detail: the reluc-
tant Lot, his wife wringing her hands and looking back
over her shoulder, and the daughters making away
unconcernedly towards the right with pack-mule and
little dog, while on the left the avenging angels have set
about the destruction of the city 'with fire and brimstone'.

39. ABRAHAM ENTERTAINING THE ANGELS. Genesis XVIII. 8–12. Etching by Rembrandt. Dated 1656.
Three men stand before Abraham in the Hain Mamre and he invites them in, 'and set before them, and he stood by them under the tree, and they did eat' (Genesis XVIII. 8). The three men are squatting cross-legged around a platter; the middle one, without wings (the other two have angels' wings) holds a goblet and is talking with the bowing, deferential Abraham standing below him, who has placed a jug by him on the parapet. The three 'men' have a strange look. Rembrandt used an Indian miniature (now in the British Museum, London) as model for this group, deliberately adopting foreign features to characterize the supernatural and the divine. Sarah stands behind the door listening to the conversation, amused at the promise of a son in her advanced old age. The boy bending over the parapet and shooting with bow and arrow is Ishmael, the 'wild' son of Hagar.

40. THE DISMISSAL OF HAGAR. Genesis XXI. 14. Engraving by Lucas van Leyden. About 1508.
The text says Abraham gives the two outcasts 'bread, and a bottle of water' to take with them. Ishmael carries the bread before him and Hagar is just receiving a jug. Sarah, with the young Isaac standing by her side, sits against the courtyard wall watching the departure that she has brought about.

41. SARAH COMPLAINING OF HAGAR TO ABRAHAM. Genesis XXI. 10–11. Pen and ink drawing by Rembrandt in the Louvre, Paris. About 1640.
An episode seldom illustrated, preceding the dismissal. 'Cast out this bondwoman and her son: for the son of this bondwoman shall not be heir with my son, even with Isaac,' Sarah says to Abraham. The aged Sarah and the young Hagar are in marked contrast to each other and the back view of Abraham seems to convey that 'the thing was very grievous in Abraham's sight' (Genesis XXI. 11).

42. THE DISMISSAL OF HAGAR. Genesis XXI. 14. Painting by Rembrandt in the Victoria and Albert Museum, London. Dated 1640.
This unusual presentation of the theme was originally devised as a 'Flight into Egypt' and then transformed by Rembrandt himself into a 'Dismissal of Hagar'. This explains the ass in the picture. The young Ishmael leads the beast, round which the water-bottle is hung prominently. Abraham, venerable, old and bent, stands close by with a vague gesture of farewell.

43. THE DISMISSAL OF HAGAR. Genesis XXI. 14. Painting by Jan Steen in the Staatliche Gemäldegalerie, Dresden. About 1660.
Hagar, in tears, the water-bottle hanging over her arm, takes leave of the troubled old man on the steps of the house. In the arch of the doorway sits Sarah with the laughing Isaac in her lap. In the foreground the young Ishmael equips himself with bow and arrow for the journey, obviously an indication that Ishmael 'will be a wild man; his hand will be against every man, and every man's hand against him' (Genesis XVI. 12).

44. HAGAR AND THE ANGEL AT THE FOUNTAIN. Genesis XVI. 6–14. Painting by Ferdinand Bol in the Rijksmuseum, Amsterdam. About 1665.
This shows the promise made to Hagar when she was carrying Ishmael and when, threatened by Sarah, she had fled into the wilderness, where the Angel of the Lord appeared to her by the fountain and bid her return and submit; she would bear a son, whom she should call Ishmael, and his seed would multiply and it would not be numbered for multitude.

45. ABRAHAM'S SACRIFICE. Genesis XXII. 9–11. Marble Statue by Donatello and Nanni di Bartolo, from the east side of the Campanile in Florence. 1421. Now in the Museo di S. Maria del Fiore, Florence.
As prescribed by the Florentine tradition, the father has seized the hair of his kneeling son, whose hands are tied behind his back, and has laid the short knife on his shoulder. Abraham, his sleeve rolled back ready for the deed, turns round upon hearing the angel call.

46. ABRAHAM'S SACRIFICE. Genesis XXII. 9–11. Statue from the right jamb of the middle portal in the North transept of Chartres Cathedral. About 1230.
At first glance not unlike the Donatello figure, but upon closer examination decisive differences appear, not only in the artist's temperament but also in the iconographical treatment. The boy, his feet bound and hands crossed before his body, is *standing* upright and the father has laid his left hand almost tenderly upon his neck, whilst in his right he holds the (broken-off) sword high above shoulder-level. This Abraham is no single statue but belongs to a row of sculptures on either side of a porchway, one statue amongst others; he is flanked by Moses and Melchisedek. Thus the artist can bring more figures into the story than was possible for Donatello with his isolated statue. The base of the figure is decorated with the ram to be sacrificed in place of the son, and the Angel (not visible in our illustration) with a banderol comes forward out of the baldaquin over Melchisedek's head and leans over towards Abraham in warning and admonition.

47. ABRAHAM'S SACRIFICE. Genesis XXII. 9–11. Etching by Rembrandt. Signed and dated 1655.
Isaac is not, as described in the Bible, laid 'on the altar upon the wood', but resting over the knee of his father,

THE SPIRIT OF GOD MOVING OVER THE FACE OF THE WATERS.
English Miniature, about 1050. London, British Museum (MS. Tib. VI, fol. 7v).

who covers his son's eyes with his left hand. This would seem to be a development of the affectionate gesture of Abraham in Chartres Cathedral. A large flat vessel to collect up the blood of the sacrifice stands before Abraham. The 'call' of the angel is here a very real 'intervention'. The angel puts his arms from behind around the startled Abraham and literally stays his hand. The huge wings of the angel overshadow the whole group.

48. ABRAHAM'S SACRIFICE. Genesis XXII. 9–11. Painting by Rembrandt in the Hermitage, Leningrad. Signed and dated 1635.
Between the etching on the opposite page and this picture there lies a gap of exactly twenty years. The differences in conception and execution are enormous, from the torso of Isaac, bent uncomfortably backward, to the angel flying, storming down, and the knife slipping from the hand of Abraham – everything in the oil painting of the twenty-nine year old is set forth in extremely dramatic fashion. And yet, already there are features in it, which are repeated with different intent in the etching of the forty-nine year old, e.g. the left hand of Abraham carefully covering the face of his son and the advancing angel who, not content with calling, actually stretches out a hand to prevent the sacrifice taking place. In the whole history of art there are but few examples in which the development of an outstanding personality from tempestuous youth to temperate old age can so clearly be traced.

49. ELIEZER AND REBEKAH AT THE WELL; REBEKAH WATERING ELIEZER'S CAMELS Genesis XXIV. Marginal illustration by the so-called 'Maître de Boqueteaux' in the French Bible of Jean de Sy, Paris, Bibliothèque Nationale MS. fr. 15397, fol. 40 verso. About 1356.

Two scenes, exactly as described in the text: first Rebekah gives Eliezer water from the pitcher and then she waters his camels. There are only two camels, not ten, as the Bible says, and the 'goods of his master' take the form of wooden chests, strapped to the backs of the animals. The well is a fountain springing up from below the little tree-covered hill.

50. REBEKAH WATERING ELIEZER'S CAMELS; THE JOURNEY OF REBEKAH AND ELIEZER. Genesis XXIV. 19–20 and 61. Mosaic in the nave (North wall) of Monreale, Palermo. Last third of the 12th century.
At Monreale the overwhelming rich decoration includes a complete cycle of the Old Testament in the nave – from the Creation to Jacob and the Angel – carried out in all probability by Greek mosaicists summoned to Sicily. Eliezer, this time accompanied by two servants, looks on with a gesture of astonishment, while Rebecca gives the camels water from a trough shaped like an antique sarcophagus. And then she follows Eliezer to the land of Abraham; they use the camels as mounts with one servant leading and the other behind.

51. REBEKAH GIVING WATER TO ELIEZER AND HIS CAMELS. Genesis XXIV. 17–20. Miniature from the Vienna Genesis, Cod. Purpur. Vindob. Graec. 31, fol. VII, p. 13. Vienna, Staatsbibliothek. Middle of the 6th century.
A walled city on the right from which Rebekah, with the pitcher – an antique clay vessel – on her shoulder, descends to the well. The street, too, looks quite antique, marked by milestones. The woman reclining by the water is the personification of the Nymph. Next, Rebekah is standing in the foreground, her foot resting on the edge of the well, giving Eliezer a drink from her pitcher, while the camels – this time there are a considerable number – are already helping themselves from the trough by the well.

52. REBEKAH RECEIVING THE JEWELS FROM ELIEZER'S MASTER; REBEKAH RELATING WHAT BEFELL HER BY THE WELL. Genesis XXIV. 22 and 23–31. Miniature from the Vienna Genesis, Cod. Purpur. Vindob. Graec. 31, fol. VII, p. 14 (see No. 51). Middle of the 6th century.
The subsequent scene is again in two strips: above, the Nymph lying by the spring as before. Abraham's servant speaks with Rebekah, and 'as the camels had done drinking, . . . (he) took a golden earring of half a shekel weight and two bracelets for her hands'. Eliezer, above, between the Nymph and the resting camels, is about to fasten on the bracelet. Below, on the right, in the house, implied by a door and its surrounds, Rebekah tells her parents what has happened to her at the well, whilst in the bottom left-hand corner her mother – as is clear from the colouring of the clothes in the original – is talking with Eliezer.

53. ELIEZER AND REBEKAH. Genesis XXIV. 22–25. Painting by Nicolas Poussin in the Louvre, Paris. 1648.
Poussin has chosen the moment when the bodily needs of man and beast have been met, and Abraham's servant speaks with the daughter of Bethuel. In his left hand, he holds a purse containing the presents. He is dressed in 'oriental' fashion, i.e. he wears turban and scimitar and a quiver of arrows is strapped around him. The well is beautifully built of stone '. . . without the city (where) the daughters of the men come out to draw water' (Genesis XXIV. 13) and the most amazing feature of the picture, when we compare it with the earlier representations, is the vast number of maidens gathered there. A comparison between this picture in the classical vein, which strives towards historical accuracy in decor and detail, and the genuinely antique version in the Vienna Genesis, is altogether very revealing.

54. REBEKAH AND ELIEZER. Genesis XXIV. 17–18. Painting by Murillo in the Prado, Madrid. About 1668.
Murillo, in contrast to the richness and elegance of Poussin's city girls, returns to the simplicity and innocence of shepherd life. A draw-well, in need of repair, stands on a height, around which four country maidens are gathered; in the background on the left, the caravan with the camels. Rebekah is offering a drink from a copper vessel to the thirsty Eliezer, whose massive silhouette is outlined against the sky. With a questioning look she is turning round at her companions.

55. ISAAC BLESSING JACOB. Genesis XXVII. 18–29. Painting by Gerbrandt van den Eeckhout. Metropolitan Museum, New York. Signed and dated 1642.
Jacob has disguised himself as a hunter with a quiver over his shoulder, bow at his side, and skin gauntlet over hands and arms, in order to make his father believe he is Esau and that he has killed the game for him. Rebekah, who had thought of the ruse stands imperiously at his side; through the door behind on the left Esau is returning home with his kill.

56. ISAAC BLESSING JACOB. Genesis XXVII. 18–29. Painting by Murillo in the Hermitage, Leningrad. About 1670.
Jacob obtaining the blessing under false pretences, has his mother Rebekah by his side, who has not only goaded him into this deception, but stands by him while he carries out her scheme. From the distant hilly landscape Esau emerges, returning with his hounds from the hunt.

57. JACOB'S DREAM. Genesis XXVIII. 11-15. Painting by Domenico Feti in the Kunsthistorisches Museum, Vienna. About 1616.

Jacob's vision during his flight offered the painter plenty of scope for individual interpretation. Feti puts the young Jacob well in the foreground, worn out from his wanderings; dog, staff and bundle by his side, a pair of stone steps for his pillow. These steps go right up to the low hanging clouds, which open to show '. . . the angels . . . ascending and descending on it'.

58-59. JACOB TENDING LABAN'S FLOCKS; JACOB'S DREAM. Genesis XXVIII. 11-15 and XXIX. 20. Paintings by Ribera. 58 in the Museo Cerralbo and 59 in the Prado, Madrid. About 1639.

Jacob, a bearded young man holding a lamb on his lap, a large flock grazing about him, sits in the shade of a tree and looks up, as if he had heard a call.

Jacob lies stretched out sleeping, while behind the heavens have opened and a number of tiny angels climb up and down in the blaze of light. The two pictures were painted as counter-pieces.

60. JACOB'S DREAM. Genesis XXVIII. 11-15. Painting by Murillo in the Hermitage, Leningrad. About 1670.

An exhausted wanderer – a bearded, mature man – Jacob lies propped on his arm, with water-bottle, bundle and staff by his side. It is night. The moon, half-hidden by clouds, rides in the sky. And there stands 'a ladder', as described in the text, reaching right up to heaven, with six angels climbing up and down on it.

61. JACOB'S DREAM. Genesis XXVIII. 11-15. Fresco by Raphael and Baldassare Peruzzi on the ceiling of the Stanza d'Eliodoro in the Vatican, Rome. About 1512-14.

This is one of four scenes from the Old Testament decorating the circular ceiling. The three others are: God appearing to Noah, Abraham's Sacrifice and God appearing to Moses in the Burning Bush (see Note 96). This segment of a circle with its irregular shape is used to the greatest advantage in the diagonal composition. The sleeping Jacob, a fully-grown, bearded man, with two stones as pillows, cradling his head in his arms, lies apart to the left of the vision; a stairway ascends parallel with the frame, encircled by clouds, and God himself appears in the heavens with arms stretched wide in a gesture of blessing.

62. RECONCILIATION OF JACOB AND ESAU. Genesis XXXIII. 3-16. Painting by Rubens in the Alte Pinakothek, Munich. About 1625-27.

Esau, a warrior in arms, approaches with his army from the left; helmeted followers with their horses accompany him. Jacob on the right bows before him; a group of his kinsfolk cluster around him, including the handmaidens Bilhah and Zilpah with their children, cattle and herdsmen between them and camels at their back – part of the riches Jacob had acquired in alien lands.

63. JOSEPH TELLING HIS DREAM. Genesis XXXVII. 9-10. Grisaille sketch by Rembrandt for an etching (dated 1638) in the Rijksmuseum, Amsterdam, dated 163(?).

The scene is laid indoors. Jacob sits at Leah's bed-side, the brothers stand at the foot, and Joseph faces the old couple, relating his dream, unaware of the bitterness and envy that his tale is stirring up among his brothers behind his back.

64, 65, 70, 71, 81. Five scenes from the Story of Joseph. From the Cupola mosaic of the Baptistery, S. Giovanni, Florence. Last third of the 13th century.

After the Creation cycle in the cupola of the Baptistery, there follows a comprehensive series dealing with the Story of Joseph, in fifteen separate scenes, beginning with his dreams.

64. JOSEPH IS LIFTED FROM THE PIT AND SOLD TO THE ISHMAELITES. Genesis XXXVII. 38.

This is the fourth in the series; the brothers are lifting Joseph out of the pit, to sell him for 'twenty pieces of silver' to the Midianites passing that way. The nearest old man is just handing over a purse to the brother who stands directly behind Joseph. The seventeen-year-old Joseph still wears his 'coat of many colours', or, at least, a much richer and finer one than any of his brothers.

65. JOSEPH WITH THE MIDIANITES ON THEIR WAY TO EGYPT. Genesis XXXVII. 28. (See No. 64.)

Joseph, divested of his bright robe, in a short traveller's coat with his staff over his shoulders, strides along with two of the men and turns to the two following behind him.

66. JACOB RECEIVING THE BLOOD-STAINED COAT OF JOSEPH. Genesis XXXVII. 31-33. Painting by Velazquez in the Escorial, Madrid. About 1630.

This is the only Old Testament picture by Velazquez and has a mythological scene, The Forge of Vulcan, as a companion piece. There are five brothers recounting their dreadful news to the elderly Jacob. It is an open hall, in whose shade the old man sits; two brothers stand uneasily, silhouetted against the bright background; two have produced the blood-stained evidence; a fifth stands with his back to the viewer and covers his eyes with his hand to shut out the sight. The old father has dropped his stick and raised his hands in horror.

67. JACOB RECEIVING THE BLOODSTAINED COAT OF JOSEPH. Genesis XXXVII. 31–33.

Italian painting of the 17th century in the Samuel H. Kress Collection. Washington, National Gallery of Art.

Four of the brothers burst in upon the old man sitting in his chair and show him the garment; he recoils in horror and turns away from the ghastly sight. Behind Jacob stands the young Benjamin, who has remained in the house, and is therefore ignorant of the crime.

68. JOSEPH AND POTIPHAR'S WIFE. Genesis XXXIX. 11–12. English miniature from the Munich Psalter. Clm. 835, fol. 14 recto (below). Staatsbibliothek, Munich. Before 1222.

The seduction scene is played out before two arcades; Potiphar's wife holds Joseph's coat tight in her hand, and he is just trying to slip out of it, pulling it off with both hands. That he will successfully escape, can be gathered from the fact that his right leg has already disappeared behind the frame.

69. POTIPHAR'S WIFE ACCUSING JOSEPH. Genesis XXXIX. 14–18. Miniature from the Vienna Genesis (see Nos. 51, 52), Cod. Purpur, Vindob. Grac. 31, fol. XVI, p. 32. Middle of the 6th century.

Like the previous illustrations from this manuscript, this is in two strips; above: Potiphar's wife, elegantly dressed, sitting on a folding stool, calls 'unto the men of her house', and makes her charge. Below, she stands wearing the same rich dress with a veil over her head, and a serving maid at her side holds out the coat, and shows it to the group standing before her.

70. JOSEPH IS SOLD INTO THE HOUSE OF POTIPHAR. Genesis XXXIX. I. Mosaic from the cupola in the Baptistery, S. Giovanni, Florence. Last third of the 13th century (see Nos. 64, 65).

Potiphar in a turban-like head-dress indicating his high rank as 'officer of Pharaoh . . . and captain of the guard', sits in an elegant, antique open hall, hung with garlands. Behind him stands his wife who seems to be addressing him. Potiphar concludes the bargain by shaking hands with Joseph, the young man standing before him. Behind him are two of the Ishmaelites who have brought him to Egypt.

71. JOSEPH IS CAST INTO PRISON. Genesis XXXIX. 20. (See above Nos. 64, 65 and 70.)

Potiphar's wife, the cause of the trouble, stands in the door of the house behind her husband, whom she seems to be pushing forward with both hands. Joseph, falsely accused, is being led away by two men. Potiphar himself – easily recognizable once more by his magnificent head-dress – sends him off to prison with words of warning as he goes.

72. JOSEPH IN EGYPT. Genesis XXXVII. 28 and XLI, 48–49, 56; XLIV. 12–13; XLV. 14. Bronze relief from the third door, the so-called 'Porta del Paradiso' in the Baptistery of S. Giovanni, Florence, by Lorenzo Ghiberti. About 1430–40 (see Nos. 11, 20, 29).

From the story of Joseph, so rich in incident, Ghiberti chooses his activities in Egypt. He therefore begins at the top on the right, in the flattest relief, with the sale of Joseph to the Ishmaelites. The whole of the centre is taken up by a circular Renaissance building, open to the sky, one of the 'cornhouses', into which 'Joseph gathered corn as the sand of the sea, very much, until he left numbering' (Genesis XLI. 49) and later sold it from these stores. On the right is a group of Egyptians, while on the left the story of Benjamin is being unfolded (see No. 76).

73–74. Two ivory plaques from the Maximian Cathedra formerly in the Cathedral of Ravenna, now in the Archiepiscopal Museum; from the middle of the 6th century, possibly originating from Ravenna itself; the Joseph scenes show an Alexandrine influence. The story of Joseph is depicted in ten panels, five on each of the outer sides of the two arm-rests of the cathedra.

73. JOSEPH DISTRIBUTING CORN IN EGYPT. Genesis XLI. 56 and XLII. 25.

It is not perfectly clear whether the corn is here being sold to the Egyptians or to the brothers of Joseph. At any rate it is clear that Joseph, in imperial array, is supervising the distribution from his throne with cushions and foot-rest, behind which stand two attendants. Close by, a scribe notes down on a tablet the amount handed over.

74. MEETING OF JOSEPH AND JACOB. Genesis XLVI. 29–30.

Joseph in imperial robes, as before, embraces the old man who bows before him; behind Joseph four Egyptian soldiers of his retinue; behind Jacob three brothers, shepherds with their crooks, all raising their hands in amazement.

75. JACOB LETS BENJAMIN DEPART FOR EGYPT WITH HIS BRETHREN. Genesis XLIII. 8–15. Painting by Barent Fabritius in the Mauritshuis, The Hague. About 1655.

The parting words of the aged Israel, whose left hand still rests upon the shoulders of the youthful Benjamin, and who bids his son farewell with a heavy heart. Close to Israel stands Judah, who has stood surety for the boy, and another of the brothers, with his back to us. The resemblance between the old man Israel and the young Benjamin is rather touching.

76. THE SILVER CUP IS FOUND IN BENJAMIN'S SACK; JOSEPH REVEALS HIMSELF TO HIS BRETHREN. Genesis XLIV. 12 and XLV. 1–14. Detail of Plate 72.
On the left a crowd of Egyptians, recognizable by their turbans and fezes, one of whom, in their midst, points reproachfully at the cup in Benjamin's sack. Benjamin stands to the right of it, a little figure with arms outspread in protest and behind him the brothers in despair; the foremost one – presumably Reuben – rending his garments; another buries his head in his arms, three of them stretch out their hands pleadingly – beseechingly to the Egyptians, three more clutch their heads in anguish. Then above it on a balcony, the recognition scene between the brothers, or rather between the two sons of Rachel, little Benjamin and Joseph, the great ruler, clasping each other in close embrace. In this flat background relief all twelve brothers are clearly present, exactly as described in the text.

77. POTIPHAR'S WIFE ACCUSING JOSEPH. Genesis XXXIX. 13–18. Detail of a painting by Rembrandt, formerly in the Hermitage, Leningrad, now in the National Gallery, Washington. Signed and dated 1655.
In the half light of Potiphar's bed-chamber, the woman is sitting on a chair near the bed, clutching her garments closely around her with her left hand, while she points accusingly with her right at Joseph behind the bed. He does not defend himself, but stands there silently with hands folded, a bunch of keys at his girdle as his sign of office. Potiphar, richly clad in oriental fashion, listens to his wife's accusation also in silence, with his right arm leaning on the back of her chair.

78. JACOB BLESSING EPHRAIM AND MANASSEH. Genesis XLVIII. 10–19. Painting by Rembrandt in the Staatliche Gemäldegalerie, Cassel. Dated 1656.
'Israel strengthened himself and sat upon the bed' (Genesis XLVIII. 2) and blessed the younger grandson Ephraim with his right hand and laid his left hand on the head of the elder one Manasseh. Joseph who stands behind him, in a heavy turban, 'held up his father's hand, to remove it from Ephraim's head unto Manasseh's head' (Genesis XLVIII. 17), 'And his father refused' (Genesis XLVIII. 19). A little way apart from this closely knit group stands Joseph's wife Asenath, the daughter of the priest of On, the mother of the sons, an Egyptian.

79. JACOB LETS BENJAMIN DEPART FOR EGYPT WITH HIS BRETHREN; JOSEPH REVEALS HIMSELF TO HIS BRETHREN. Genesis XLIII. 8–15. English miniature from the Munich Psalter. Clm. 835 fol. 16 recto, Staatsbibliothek, Munich. Before 1222 (see No. 68).

Above: Jacob entrusts Benjamin to the brothers. The old man sits wringing his hands, while Benjamin stands before him, holding Judah's hand with his right. They are ready for the journey; the two asses are loaded.
Below: Joseph has risen from his throne and embraces his brother Benjamin, causing his mantle to spread itself around him protectingly. The others look on with amazement.

80. JACOB'S JOURNEY INTO EGYPT. Genesis XLVI. 5. Miniature from the Stiftsbibliothek, Admont (Austria), Cod. 1, fol. 27 verso, formerly at Admont, now in the Vienna Staatsbibliothek. About 1130–50.
The aged Jacob in a pointed Jewish hat, a woman at his side, stands on the two-wheeled wagon which Joseph had sent; and in this manner he travels down to Egypt to his son Joseph, led by another of his sons, who is hitching the two horses by the bridle.

81. MEETING OF JACOB AND JOSEPH IN GOSHEN. Genesis XLVI. 29. Mosaic from the Baptistery S. Giovanni, Florence (see Nos. 64, 65, 70, 71). Last third of the 13th century.
This is the last of the fifteen in the series of mosaics setting out the story of Joseph in the second circle of the cupola in the Baptistery. It illustrates quite literally Genesis XLVI. 29 – 'And Joseph made ready his chariot, and went up to meet Israel his father . . . and he fell on his neck and wept on his neck a good while'. Israel approaches from the right, Joseph from the left. Horses and wagon wheels suggest the carriages and behind them the two stand embracing one another.

82. JOSEPH AS VICEROY RECEIVES HIS BROTHERS UNRECOGNIZED AND IS MOVED TO TEARS. Genesis XLII. 24–26. Greek miniature from the Vienna Genesis, Cod. Purpur. Vindob. Graec. 31, fol. XIX, p. 37 (see Nos. 51, 52, 69). Middle of the 6th century.
The brothers' first journey to Egypt; Joseph, who understands what they are saying, has turned away from them, unmanned by his emotion, that is to say, he has left by the door on the right and is weeping, his mantle over his face. Then he reappears by the door on the left and orders Simeon to be bound, which an Egyptian is about to do, while five brothers are bending over sacks and the others stand around in a group.

83. THE BURIAL OF JACOB. Genesis L. 7–13. Detail of a full-page illumination with the story of Joseph, Ashburnham Pentateuch, Paris, Bibliothèque Nationale, nouv. acq. lat. 2334, fol. 50 recto. 7th century.
Joseph had his father embalmed and then bound up like an Egyptian mummy by Egyptian doctors; three men are bearing Jacob into the 'double cave'; into the family

burial-place before Mamre, which Abraham had bought and where a second tomb is erected inside a natural cave. Before it is the bier, on which Joseph's people had transported the body of Jacob to Mamre. Behind this stands Joseph with an 'elder' and other followers.

84–86. THE STORY OF JOSEPH. Ivory reliefs in three strips from a byzantine casket. 12th century. 84 and 85 in the Kaiser Friedrich Museum in Berlin, 86 in the British Museum, London.

84. JOSEPH IS SENT BY JACOB TO HIS BRETHREN IN DOTHEN; JOSEPH IS SOLD BY HIS BRETHREN TO THE ISHMAELITES. Genesis XXXVII. 13–17 and 28.
On the left is the scene, illustrated comparatively rarely, in which Jacob sends the young Joseph away to his brothers; this is linked directly with the meeting between Joseph and 'a man' when he has lost his way (Genesis XXXVII. 15–17). The 'man' in this version is an angel, a guardian angel, leading the way for Joseph. Then hard upon this comes the sale of Joseph to the Ishmaelites; in the centre Joseph is being hauled stark naked out of the pit and on the far right he is sitting on a camel-like horse on his way to Egypt.

85. JOSEPH IN EGYPT; THE MEETING OF JACOB AND JOSEPH. Genesis XLV. 20–24; XLVI. 29.
Joseph in crown and imperial mantle watches the corn being distributed to the brothers on the left; then next we see him sending a wagon, in this case with a yoke of oxen, to fetch his father (centre) and finally on the far right the reunion with Jacob in which father and long-lost son embrace one another.

86. JACOB BLESSING EPHRAIM AND MANASSEH; THE DEATH OF JACOB. Genesis XLVIII. 13–14; XLIX. 33; L. I.
Jacob sits in complete full-face and has crossed his hands so that he is blessing the younger Ephraim with his right, while he lays his left hand on the head of the older and distinctly taller Manasseh. Then on the right, beautifully laid out, the body of Jacob, and Joseph, in crown and robes of state as before, 'fell upon his father's face, and wept upon him, and kissed him'.

87–89. Three scenes from the story of Moses on the so-called Lipsanoteca in Brescia. Ivory relief from a casket once in the S. Giulia, now in the Museo Civico Cristiano, Brescia. About 310–20, closely akin to sarcophagi of the 4th century, possibly from Asia Minor or of Western origin.

87. THE FINDING OF MOSES. Exodus II. 5–6.
Reduced to a minimum: three women, the foremost one in rich clothes is the Princess, Pharaoh's daughter. She points with a commanding gesture towards a shallow platter, on which lies the baby Moses wrapped in swaddling clothes.

88. MOSES SLAYING THE EGYPTIAN. Exodus II. 11–12.
Like the previous scene, reduced to the bare essentials: the Egyptian sinking to the ground is finished off by a hefty kick from Moses.

89. 'BREAD OF PROVIDENCE,' MOSES TAKEN INTO THE HOUSE OF JETHRO. Exodus II. 20–21.
This relief has given rise to various interpretations: the latest and most plausible one is that it represents the meal in the house of Jethro. Jethro is speaking to his daughters, who have told him of the Egyptian who helped them. 'Where is he? Why is it that ye have left the man? Call him that he may eat bread' (Exodus II. 20). Five men are seated around a table laid with a small loaf before each of them and a chicken on the platter in the centre. A servant on the left busies himself with a huge cauldron over a log fire.

90. THE FINDING OF MOSES. Exodus II. 3–9.
Painting by Giambattista Tiepolo in the National Gallery of Scotland, Edinburgh. About 1755–60.
On the palm-studded banks of the Nile stands the daughter of Pharaoh with her retinue of ladies-in-waiting, pages and dogs; on the extreme right, the reed basket, out of which the child has been lifted. The two women, the younger one bending eagerly over it, and the older one holding it lovingly against her breast, are probably Moses' sister and mother. 'Then said his sister to Pharoah's daughter, shall I go and call to thee a nurse of the Hebrew women, that she may nurse the child for thee? And Pharoah's daughter said to her: Go. And the maid went and called the child's mother' (Exodus II. 7–8).

91. THE FINDING OF MOSES. Exodus II. 3–9.
Painting by Sebastien Bourdon in the Samuel H. Kress Collection, Washington, National Gallery. About 1650.
The little ark 'in the flags by the river's brink' is here the centre of attention. The princess, taller than her companions by a head, seems to be actually saying 'This is one of the Hebrews' children', as the man shows her what he has found.

92. THE FINDING OF MOSES. Exodus II. 3–9.
Painting by Paolo Veronese in the Prado, Madrid. About 1565.

Veronese dispenses with the oriental landscape, but replaces it by an oriental retinue; the servant in the left foreground removing the basket is a negro. The woman showing him to Pharaoh's daughter is probably Moses' sister. The ladies-in-waiting are standing around talking and the court atmosphere is further stressed by the dwarf in the foreground.

93. AN EPISODE FROM MOSES' YOUTH; MOSES SLAYING THE EGYPTIAN. Exodus II. 11–12. English full-page illumination from the Queen Mary Psalter, British Museum, Royal 2. B. VII, fol. 23 verso, beginning of the 14th century.

Above: A legendary story, which is not included in the Bible; how Pharaoh sets his crown upon the child and Moses snatches it from his head and throws it in the fire; then Pharaoh will have him killed unless he eats a burning coal, which he is seeking to do on the right, and is thereby reprieved.

Below: Moses – the youth on the right – hastens to the aid of one of his brethren when he is attacked by an Egyptian. The Egyptian on the right, with head-covering and an axe, is about to fall upon the Jew who is only armed with a staff, when the point of Moses' sword strikes him. Moses trips up the Jew at the same time, in order to separate them.

94. MOSES KEEPING JETHRO'S SHEEP, THE ANGEL OF THE LORD BEFORE THE BURNING BUSH, MOSES RECEIVING THE TABLES OF THE LAW. Exodus III. 1–5, XXXI. 18 and 20. A relief panel from the wooden door of S. Sabina in Rome. About 430.

The door of S. Sabina is one of the most important early Christian monuments. Eight large and ten small panels, scenes from the Old and New Testament, disarranged, and no longer in their original order, have been preserved. In this panel three episodes from the story of Moses are given, reading from top to bottom: (1) On stony ground scattered with small trees, Moses is tending the flock of his father-in-law Jethro, but is looking up to the right to the Burning Bush. (2) The Angel is standing before the bush, and is talking to Moses by his side, who has received the message and is about to take off his sandals. (3) Above Moses appears again with a companion whose arms are opened wide in astonishment, as he takes the Commandments from the hand of God into his own mantle-shrouded hands. And although this is contrary to the text, which specifically mentions 'tables', according to the antique Mediterranean tradition the Commandments are written on a scroll.

95. MOSES BEFORE THE BURNING BUSH. Exodus III. 1–6. Detail of a fresco by Botticelli in the Sistine Chapel in the Vatican, Rome. 1482.

God bends forward from the blazing bush, blessing the young Moses, kneeling before him without shoes and with a shepherd's crook, for he does in fact receive his call while watching his father-in-law's sheep. Some animals are just visible on the right.

96. GOD APPEARING TO MOSES IN THE BURNING BUSH. Exodus III. 1–6. Ceiling fresco by Raphael and Baldassare Peruzzi in the Stanza d'Eliodoro in the Vatican, Rome. About 1511–14 (see No. 61).

One of the four sections of the ceiling with representations of the Old Testament. God in flaming clouds of glory, accompanied by putti, appears to Moses who 'hid his face, for he was afraid to look upon God' (Exodus III. 6). No animals, no bush, no accessories at all, but an angel, undoubtedly the one who first spoke to Moses, seems to be drawing back the curtain of clouds. Moses, although no animals are there, can be recognized as a shepherd by his crook and pouch.

97–100. Four frescoes by Bernardino Luini from a richly decorated villa, once in the Casa di Campagna of the Pelucchi family in Monza, now in the Brera, Milan. About 1522.

97. THE SLAYING OF THE FIRST-BORN. Exodus XII. 12 and 29.

The morning after the night that the Lord smote all the first-born in Egypt; a broad landscape with dead birds and cattle, with men and women lamenting in the background, while in the foreground grief-stricken mothers throw themselves upon their dead children, clutch them to their breasts or call heaven to witness with arms upraised: 'And there was a great cry in all Egypt' (Exodus XII. 30).

98. THE CHILDREN OF ISRAEL PREPARE TO DEPART FROM EGYPT. Exodus XII. 33–37.

In contrast to the Egyptians bewailing their dead, the Israelite women here are happy with their children, while the men make ready for the departure: bundles are tied, camels and mules laden and in the background the people are assembling ready to leave the country.

99. THE DESTRUCTION OF PHARAOH'S HOST. Exodus XIV. 5–9 and 23–28.

Pharaoh sets out after the Israelites with 'six hundred chosen chariots', but the Lord 'troubled the host of the Egyptians. And took off their chariot wheels, so that they drove them heavily.' The fresco by Luini is an exact illustration of the passage: chariots overturning, men and beasts drowning in profusion, among them an elephant in full panoply bearing three of the leaders; all are swirled away by the waters.

100. THE DELIVERANCE OF THE ISRAEL-ITES. Exodus XIV. 21–22 and 26–29.

The Israelites have crossed the Red Sea on dry ground, and have made good their escape onto the other side where Moses stands with upraised staff and obeys the word of God 'Stretch out thine hand over the sea, that the waters may come again upon the Egyptians, upon their chariots and upon their horsemen' (Exodus XIV. 26), which is exactly what is happening to the left. Aaron by Moses' side is pointing to the scene of the disaster: in the very foreground on the shore, stands a woman only half visible – Miriam, the prophetess.

101. SCENES FROM THE YOUTH OF MOSES. Exodus II. 11–19; III. 4–10; XII. 37–38. Fresco by Botticelli in the Sistine Chapel in the Vatican, Rome. 1482.

Moses occurs seven times in this fresco tracing the story of his youth up to the time of the exodus from Egypt. In the right foreground he bends with drawn sword over a terror-stricken Egyptian and kills him. Directly behind this, he is fleeing into the desert, an outcast, his back turned towards the viewer with a staff over his shoulder. In the centre, by the draw-well under the trees on the right, with upraised staff, he is driving away the shepherds who are molesting Jethro's daughter; then he waters their sheep at the trough, while two of Jethro's daughters look on. On the hill top, framed by trees, sits Moses, who has heard the Lord's command and is taking off his shoes. To the left he talks with God in the Burning Bush (see No. 95); and then in the foreground below, right against the left border, he is seen again, striding along, leading the people of Israel out of Egypt.

102. MOSES RETURNING TO EGYPT WITH HIS WIFE ZIPPORAH AND HIS TWO SONS; THE CIRCUMCISION OF ELIEZER. Exodus IV. 18–25. Fresco by Pinturicchio in the Sistine Chapel in the Vatican, Rome. 1481–3.

These incidents are rarely illustrated; here, too, Moses appears several times over in a continuous narrative. The sequence of events begins in the middle distance, towards the back, where Moses is taking leave of his father-in-law Jethro. From there the train of the Moses family with servants and serving maids, pack-laden camels, and dogs, curves forward on the left. Moses has just reached the middle foreground; on his left, his wife Zipporah with two sons Gershom and Eliezer; and the Lord in the guise of an angel came to meet him and tried to kill him. 'Then Zipporah took a sharp stone and cut off the foreskin of her son and cast it at his feet and said, "Surely a bloody husband art thou to me"' (Exodus IV. 25), which is happening in the right-hand corner. Moses, recognizable by his staff ('And thou shalt take this rod in thine hand, wherewith thou shalt do signs') (Exodus IV. 17) with the older son Gershom at his side, watches the ceremony.

103. THE CROSSING OF THE RED SEA (THE DESTRUCTION OF PHARAOH'S HOST). Exodus XIV. 23–31; XV. 20–21. Fresco by Cosimo Rosselli in the Sistine Chapel in the Vatican, Rome. 1481–3.

In the background on the right is Pharaoh's city and Pharaoh before his palace surrounded by his servants (Exodus XIV. 5). They are deciding to pursue the Israelites. Then in the foreground the annihilation takes place: a dense mass of horsemen and chariots is being swallowed up in the swirling tides; the pillar of fire ahead and the cloud above, which 'troubled the host of the Egyptians' (Exodus XIV. 24). On the shore stand the Israelites who have escaped, Moses with his rod at their head, behind him Aaron, identified by his calotte and sacramental vessel. At the other side of Moses kneels Miriam, the prophetess, Aaron's sister, who accompanies her song of praise on a triangular instrument.

104. THE CROSSING OF THE RED SEA. Exodus XIV. 23–31. Painting by Lucas Cranach in the Alte Pinakothek, Munich. Signed and dated 1530.

On the left stand the Israelites massed shoulder to shoulder 'six thousand on foot that were men, beside children' (Exodus XII. 37), first and foremost Moses with his rod, and Aaron at his side with a censer; an angel stands before them, bringing them the Word of God (Exodus XIV. 1–4). And behind them his prophecy has already come to pass: 'the six hundred chosen chariots and captains of Egypt' (Exodus XIV. 7) are drowning in the Red Sea, which has foamed up into a gigantic wave, forming at the same time a protective wall for the Israelites.

105. THE GATHERING OF THE MANNA. Exodus XVI. 13–16. Painting by Tintoretto in S. Giorgio Maggiore, Venice. About 1591–4.

This is not the first gathering of the manna which saved the people from starvation, but one of the untold harvest that came later, for 'the children of Israel did eat manna forty years, until they came to a land inhabited; they did eat manna unto the borders of the land of Canaan' (Exodus XVI. 35). This is an ordinary day in the life of the people in the wilderness, where they are busy washing, spinning, cobbling; some are engaged in the search for manna. Moses sits towards the front in the right-hand corner and is talking with Aaron. 'The skin of his face shone' (Exodus XXXIV. 29), which means that this must be after he received the Covenant on Mount Sinai.

106. THE GATHERING OF THE MANNA. Exodus XVI. 13–16. Painting by Nicolas Poussin in the Louvre, Paris. About 1639.

The whole tribe is on the verge of dying of hunger; a woman in the left foreground offers the breast to another grown woman; they all look upward to see if their salvation will come. Among them, standing erect and

MOSES ON MOUNT SINAI. Woodcut by
Hans Holbein.

thrown up in relief by dark cliffs, are Moses and Aaron.
They are promising them bread and meat, that is, quails
and manna, according to God's word; and in the right
foreground some women are already beginning to gather
up the grains of manna into shallow vessels.

107. THE GATHERING OF THE MANNA.
Exodus XVI. 13–16. Painting by Francesco Ubertini
(Bacchiacca), Samuel H. Kress Collection, National
Gallery of Art, Washington. About 1540.
The gathering of the manna is extraordinary in its exotic
touches: goats, cows and horses are all dwarfed by a
giraffe; a woman in the foreground wears a stole of tiger-
skin. This is matched by the precious salve-jars in which
the manna is being collected and the large urns on the
extreme right, in which, contrary to Moses' orders, the
manna is being stored. On the left in the background, too
large to be disregarded, rises 'the pillar of cloud' (Exodus
XIII. 21) in which the Lord went before Israel during their
forty years in the wilderness.

108. THE GATHERING OF THE MANNA.
Exodus XVI. 13–17. Painting by Dirk Bouts in St. Peter's
Church, Louvain (Belgium). Between 1464 and 1468.
One of four Old Testament scenes (the others being:
the prophet Elijah in the wilderness, the Paschal Feast,
Abraham and Melchisedek) which surround a Last
Supper. Four large figures in the foreground and a few
more scattered about in the hilly background represent
the people of Israel. Kneeling, squatting, or standing, they
are collecting the manna into small, beautifully worked
vessels, with great reverence for the wonder of it and
with the care that such treasure demands. A comparison
of Nos. 105–108 provides a glimpse of the different conceptions of 'wilderness'.

109. MOSES STRIKING WATER FROM THE
ROCK. Exodus XVII. 6. Fresco in the Catacomb of S.
Callisto, Rome. 4th century.

There are two Moses scenes illustrated in this mural:
on the left the youthful, clean-shaven Moses looses his
sandals, as the Lord has commanded from the Burning
Bush. In this case only the hand of God appears from a
corner of cloud. To the right stands an older, bearded
Moses striking water from the rock in Horeb. One man is
already quenching his thirst. This extreme simplification
enables the believer to identify himself with the event and
to see in this deliverance an assurance of his own salvation.

110. MOSES STRIKING WATER FROM THE
ROCK. Exodus XVII. 5–6. Fresco by the School of
Raphael in the Loggie in the Vatican, Rome; completed
1519.
A very faithful translation of the text into pictorial form:
the Lord hovers in a cloud of glory over the rock in
Horeb; Moses, as he was bidden, has the 'elders' with him,
who raise their arms to heaven, exulting over the stream
of water gushing out of the rock.

111. MOSES STRIKING WATER FROM THE
ROCK. Exodus XVII. 5–7. Painting by Tintoretto on the
ceiling of the Scuola di San Rocco, Venice. About 1577.
Moses stands framed by the jet of water pouring out:
before him men and women with shallow basins, only
one of them with a pitcher, press forward to collect the
water; in the very foreground on the right a woman
suckles a half-grown boy. God, after the rescue is accom-
plished, disappears in a whirl of light (above right – seen
from the back). Away to the back where the landscape
opens onto a clearing, a glimpse of the battle with the
people of Amalek (Exodus XVII. 8–13).

112. MOSES RECEIVING AND PROCLAIM-
ING THE LAW. Exodus XIX. 18–19; XXIV. 7, 13. Full-
page illumination from the Grandval Bible, London,
British Museum. Add. 10546, fol. 25 verso. School of
Tours. About 834–843.
Two scenes. *Above:* Moses receiving the tables of the
commandments from the hand of God. As on the door
of S. Sabina (see No. 94), the 'tables' are again in the form
of an antique scroll, which the hand of God reaches
down, out of a double frill of clouds. And Mount
Sinai, the clod of earth on which Moses is standing, 'was
altogether on smoke because the Lord descended upon
it in fire' (Exodus XIX. 18), sends up tongues of flame
in various places. The man by his side is Joshua. *Below:*
In a late antique open hall Moses gives out to the people
the Commandments which he holds open before him
and from which he seems to be reading. Joshua stands
behind him; the older man confronting him is probably
Aaron.

113. MOSES RECEIVING THE TABLES OF
THE LAW. Exodus XXXI. 18. Limestone relief on a stele

from Constantinople in the Kaiser Friedrich Museum, Berlin. 7th century.

The youthful Moses with knees bent receives the scroll, his hands covered reverently with his mantle. Before him a hint of Mount Sinai in the form of mounds of earth; behind him a male companion.

114. MOSES RECEIVING THE TABLES OF THE LAW. Exodus XXXI. 18. Detail of a bronze relief from the so-called 'Porta del Paradiso' by Lorenzo Ghiberti on the Baptistery of S. Giovanni, Florence. About 1436. (See Nos. 11, 20, 29, 72, 76.)

The narrow summit of the mountain gives Moses just enough room to stand on in order to receive the tables of the Commandments. Two of the angels in God's train are blowing large trumpets (Exodus XIX. 19) terrifying the people below, while Moses' servant Joshua, crouched on the mountain-side, hides his head.

115. MOSES RECEIVING THE TABLES OF THE LAW; THE WORSHIP OF THE GOLDEN CALF; MOSES BREAKING THE TABLES; HE RETURNS WITH THE NEW TABLES. Exodus XXXI. 18, XXXII and XXXIV. Fresco by Cosimo Rosselli in the Sistine Chapel in the Vatican, Rome. About 1481–83.

As in the other frescoes of this series (see Nos. 101, 102, 103) this one combines a number of events in one picture. Beginning in the centre above, where the kneeling Moses is receiving the tables of the Commandments from the hand of God (see No. 134). In the middle foreground: Moses and his servant Joshua have come down from the mountain and, on discovering what has happened (right) in his absence, Moses has started to smash the Tables of the Commandments. The Golden Calf has been erected on an altar as an idol; two men are kneeling before it in adoration. In the right foreground a young couple hold hands as they dance (Exodus XXXIV. 17–18). On a piece of bare ground towards the back, the judgement upon the children of Levi is being executed (Exodus XXXII. 27–29), 'and there fell of the people that day about three thousand men.' In the left foreground, after his second sojourn on the mountain, Moses comes down with the new tables and 'the skin of his face shone' (Exodus XXXIV. 29–30). The children of Israel are afraid of him, so the crowd is turning away from him with upraised gestures, hiding their eyes.

116. THE TENTS IN THE DESERT AND THE PILLAR OF CLOUD. Exodus XXXIII. 8–10. Fresco by the School of Raphael in the Loggie in the Vatican, Rome. Completed 1519.

Moses went and talked to the Lord in the tabernacle which he had erected; and the pillar of cloud descended and stood at the door. And the people, when they saw this, worshipped, every man in his tent door. In this fresco one man, right in front, silhouetted darkly against the open space between the tents, has fallen on his knees, whereas women with their children are standing in the doorways turned towards the pillar in their midst.

117. MOSES. Detail of a painting 'St. Luke painting the Madonna', by Jan Gossaert, called Mabuse, in the Kunsthistorisches Museum, Vienna. About 1520.

A painted statue; in a niche above the Evangelist Luke, who is engaged in drawing the Madonna in Glory, there stands a statue of the Lawgiver, who drew up The Lord's Commandments. One of the innumerable typological parallels between the Old and New Testament, in this case between the Old Testament and one of the legends of the Virgin, which have continued to influence conceptions and iconography throughout the Middle Ages and right up to the present day.

118. MOSES. Exodus XXXIV. 29–30. Marble statue by Michelangelo in S. Pietro in Vincoli, Rome. Begun about 1513, but not completed until 1542.

A statue from the Julius tomb and probably the most famous Moses figure: Moses at no particular historical moment in his life, yet a powerful figure summing up everything that the Lawgiver stands for. The horns that adorn the head of Moses here, as in many other representations (in painting and sculpture), are the result of a mistranslation of the Hebrew word for 'light' into the Latin.

119. THE COVENANT ON MOUNT SINAI; THE SETTING UP OF THE ARK OF THE COVENANT. Exodus XIX. 16 ff., and XXIV. 3 ff. Full-page illumination from the Ashburnham Pentateuch, Paris, Bibliothèque Nationale, nouv. acq. lat. 2334; 7th century. (See No. 83.)

This page must be read from top to bottom. *Above:* on the left kneels Moses, behind him Aaron, Nadab and Abihu (Exodus XXIV. 1–2). And before him God in a cloud; behind the mountain in flames. *Centre:* continuing below, the altar which Moses built for the Lord (Exodus XXIV. 4 ff.) and on which they offered sacrifice. Youths enter from the right carrying bread; on the left stands a crowd of men and women, to whom Moses, an immense figure behind the altar, holds out the tables of the Commandments and reads from it 'in the audience of the people' (Exodus XXIV). *Below:* the Tabernacle with the curtains and the table before it (Exodus XXIV. 7). Moses and Joshua stand on the left under a bright canopy, and to their right, on the opposite side: Aaron, Nadab and Abihu.

120. MOSES ON MOUNT SINAI. Exodus XIX. 16–19. Miniature from the Sarajevo Haggadah, fol. 30, a Spanish-Jewish illuminated manuscript in the Museum of Sarajevo. 14th century.

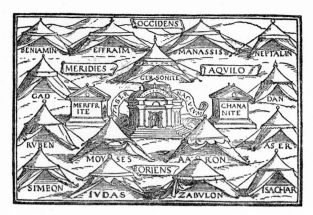

THE CHILDREN OF ISRAEL
IN THE WILDERNESS.
Woodcut by Hans Holbein.

In Heinrich Heine's words a Haggadah is 'a curious mixture of tales of our ancestors, Egyptian fables, odd stories, disputations, prayers and songs of celebration'. Moses is standing on the burning, flaming mountain; a long trumpet appears out of the wreath of clouds right over his head 'and the voice of the trumpet exceeding loud rang out so that all the people that was in the camp trembled' (Exodus XIX. 16). The mountain is encircled by people looking up and shaking.

121. THE WORSHIP OF THE GOLDEN CALF.
Exodus XXXII. 18–19. Miniature from the Admont Bible, Stiftsbibliothek, Cod. I., fol. 43 verso, now in the Staatsbibliothek, Vienna. About 1130–50. (See No. 154.)
On a richly ornamented pillar with carved capital stands the image of the animal and a group of Jews – characterized as such by their pointed Jewish hats – approach with hands outstretched in veneration. Directly before the pillar kneels a fiddle-player in illustration of Exodus XXXII. 18, 'the noise of them that sing' which Moses heard afar off as he came down from the mountain.

122. THE MESSENGERS FROM CANAAN.
Numbers XIII. Miniature from a German Weltchronik. Munich, Staatsbibliothek, Cgm. 6406, fol. 75 recto. About 1260–70.
Acting on God's instructions, Moses sends out spies into Canaan, the land which the Lord is to give to Israel. They cut down 'a branch with one cluster of grapes, and they bore it between two upon a staff' (Numbers XIII. 23), and returned with it telling the people of 'the land flowing with milk and honey' (Numbers XIII. 27). In this miniature a clear testimony to the richness of the land's fruits is given in a huge cluster of grapes which two men carry on a pole between their shoulders. The pointed hats characterize them, in the mediaeval tradition, as Jews.

123. THE REBELLION OF KORAH AND HIS TRIBE AND THEIR DESTRUCTION.
Numbers XVI. Full-page illumination by Jean Fouquet in the Antiquités et Guerres des Juifs de Josèphe, Paris, Bibliothèque Nationale. Ms. fr. 247, fol. 70. Between 1470–76.
In the foreground the battle of the Israelites against the Midianites (Numbers XXXI.). On a plateau above, the story of the rebellious faction of Korah. Korah, Dathan and Abiram rise against Moses and Aaron, but the Lord punished them, 'the ground clave asunder that was under them. And the earth opened her mouth, and swallowed them up' (Numbers XVI. 31–52). Fouquet has chosen this moment; the ground bursts as if in an earth tremor, and Korah and his followers fall into the depths. 'And all Israel that was round about fled at the cry of them: For they said, Lest the earth swallow us up also' (Numbers XVI. 34). Further back, 'two hundred and fifty men' are being consumed by tongues of fire, by the devouring flame that emanates from God in his glory. Moses, tiny and isolated on a little hill, lies on his knees, praying before the Lord.

124. THE REBELLION OF KORAH AND HIS TRIBE AND THEIR DESTRUCTION.
Numbers XVI. 18–19. Centre portion of a fresco by Botticelli in the Sistine Chapel in the Vatican, Rome. About 1481–82.
Korah's rabble railed against God and against Moses; so they were ordered to take censers and to come before the Lord with them, together with Moses and Aaron. Then God would show whose side he was on. The rebels with their censers have assembled around a fountain-like altar in front of the Constantine arch, as directed; before them stands Moses with his rod and behind them Aaron in his tiara. God's retribution must have already begun; the men let fall their censers in fright, and hold up their hands in dismay; one has already laid his face in the dust.

125. THE BRAZEN SERPENT.
Numbers XXI. 5–9. Fresco by Michelangelo in one of the spandrels on the ceiling of the Sistine Chapel, Vatican, Rome. About 1511 (see Nos. 6–9, 25, 28).
There are four spandrels in the corners of the vault of the Sistine Chapel; all four are filled with stories from the Old Testament. The others are: David killing Goliath, Judith with the head of Holofernes, and the Punishment of Haman. In his picture of the Brazen Serpent Michelangelo gives both: the punishment of the people by the fiery serpents and the healing by the brazen serpent erected by Moses. The punishment on the right takes up about two thirds of the space available. The serpents not only bite the sinners but encircle and strangle them as well. The uneven space enhances the turbulent mass of men and coiling snakes. To the left a densely packed but quiet crowd direct eyes and hands towards the brazen serpent. Moses himself is absent.

126. THE BRAZEN SERPENT. Numbers XXI. 6–9. Painting by Rubens in the National Gallery, London. About 1635–1638.

Moses and Aaron stand facing the anguished people writhing on the ground. Moses with his hands raised in admonition. Behind the two men the pole is set up, around which the brazen serpent is coiled, as on the staff of Aesculapius. Two women hold their children aloft towards the healing image. The naked man in the foreground, his mouth open in a groan, turns his eyes towards it seeking to be restored.

127. MOSES, AARON AND HUR DURING THE BATTLE OF REPHIDIM. Exodus XVII. 8–13. Miniature from a Hebrew Pentateuch. London, British Museum. Ms. Add. 11639, fol. 525 verso. Last third of the 13th century.

The three figures look very much alike and only from his position can one tell that the middle one is Moses. All three wear the same little yellow Jewish cap. Moses, not with outstretched arms (see No. 128) but with hands joined in prayer, is sitting, as described in the text, and the two others kneel by his side in order to support him. By not showing the battle itself, the illumination acquires a symbolic significance, exemplifying the power of Faith and Prayer.

128. MOSES, AARON AND HUR DURING THE BATTLE OF REPHIDIM. Exodus XVII. 8–13. Detail from a Mosaic in S. Maria Maggiore, Rome. About 432–40.

One of the Old Testament mosaics, originally 44 in number, decorating the nave of this church, comprising the earliest and most complete cycle of Old Testament scenes that have come down to us. The cycle extends from Abraham and Melchisedek to the execution of the five Amorite kings (Joshua x) (see also No. 141).

Joshua fought in the battle of Rephidim against the Amalekites; and Moses, Aaron and Hur went up onto a hill, and as long as the rod in Moses' hand stretched up towards God, the Israelites prevailed, and when he let it sink, Amalek prevailed. 'But Moses' hands were heavy', so Aaron and Hur supported his hands, one on either side of him, and Joshua won the day. Here the three stand overlooking the battle and Moses holds in his right hand the staff bestowing God's victory.

129. MOSES BLESSING THE PEOPLE; MOSES BLESSING JOSHUA. Deuteronomy XXXIII. 1 and Numbers XXVII. 18–23. Miniature from the Sarajevo Haggadah, Fol. 31 verso, a Spanish-Jewish manuscript in the Museum of Sarajevo. 14th century. (See No. 120.) Two scenes. *Above:* Moses blessing the people sitting before him, and *below:* he lays his hands upon Joshua's head, as described in the text, and ordains him to be his

successor, in the presence of the priest Eleazar and of the whole congregation.

130. BALAAM AND THE ASS. Numbers XXII. 22–31. Miniature from a German Bible. Munich, Staatsbibliothek. Cgm. 206, fol. 98 recto; Augsburg 1457.

The Angel of the Lord stands in the path of Balaam who, at the request of the Moabites, is setting out to curse the Israelites. Balaam is not aware of who it is who is coming to meet him, whereas the ass, his faithful mount, tries to step aside. But he is still ignorant of what is happening and the Lord has to open the mouth of the ass so that when it is disclosed to him verbally, Balaam is finally made to see. This moment is set forth in the simplest and most telling fashion. The ass who turns round and speaks to Balaam; Balaam threatening the animal with the whip; and the Angel of the Lord with drawn sword, who finally brings the man to his senses.

131. GOD SPEAKS TO BALAAM. Numbers XXII. 35–38. French Miniature from the Bible Moralisée. Oxford, Bodleian Library. Ms. 220, Fol. 82. About 1250 (see Nos. 132 and 173).

The so-called Bible Moralisée is one of the most richly illustrated Bibles in existence, illustrated throughout and at the same time typologized throughout. Each page carries eight miniatures set in roundels with the text in the margin next to it, four Bible scenes coupled with four interpretations of them.

Balak, the king of the Moabites, summoned Balaam so that he might curse the Israelites, but the Lord intervened and, although he allowed Balaam (on the right) to go with the princes to Moab, He ordered him to say only the words which He should put into his mouth. And so He bends low out of the clouds and touches Balaam's lips, who then proclaims to Balak in turn 'Have I now any power at all to say anything: the word that God putteth in my mouth, that shall I speak' (Numbers XXII. 38) (see No. 190, in which God bends out of the clouds over Jeremiah in a similar gesture.)

132. BALAAM'S ASS AND THE ANGEL. Numbers XXII. 22–31. See No. 131. Another miniature from the same page. About 1250.

Balaam with his whip on his stubborn ass; the animal turns around to him 'And the Lord opened the mouth of the ass, and she said unto Balaam: What have I done unto thee, that thou has smitten me three times? . . . Am I not thine ass upon which thou hast ridden ever since I was thine unto this day. . . . Then the Lord opened the eyes of Balaam, and he saw the angel of the Lord standing in the way, his sword drawn in his hand: and he bowed down his head in his hands, and fell flat on his face.' The miniaturist has succeeded in portraying all this in one small circle: the ass has fallen on one knee, its mouth open in speech, before it the huge angel with the sword, and Balaam once more bowing on bended knees before the angel.

133. THE ANGEL OF THE LORD SHOWING MOSES THE PROMISED LAND. Deuteronomy XXXIV. 1–4. Detail from a fresco by Luca Signorelli and Bartolomeo della Gatta in the Sistine Chapel in the Vatican, Rome. About 1481–83.

The arm of the angel standing behind him rests around the aged Moses, who leans on the staff conferred on him by God. He directs his gaze towards the Promised Land, promised to his people and yet denied to him. Before him lies 'all the land of Gilead unto Dan, and all Napthali, and the land of Ephraim and Manasseh, and all the land of Judah, unto the utmost sea' (Deuteronomy XXXIV. 1–2).

134. MOSES RECEIVING THE TABLES OF THE LAW. Exodus XXXII. 18. Detail of a fresco by Cosimo Rosselli in the Sistine Chapel in the Vatican, Rome. About 1481–3 (see No. 115).

After he had remained forty days and nights upon the mountain, Moses kneels with outstretched hands to receive the proffered tables of the Commandments from the hands of God. Below him sits Joshua, his minister, who has accompanied him, his head propped on his hand in meditation.

135. THE CHILDREN OF ISRAEL MOURNING OVER MOSES. Deuteronomy XXXIV. 7–8. Detail of a fresco by Luca Signorelli and Bartolomeo della Gatta in the Sistine Chapel in the Vatican, Rome. About 1481–3. (See No. 133, which is taken from the same fresco.)

Moses' 'eye was not dim, nor his natural force abated' when he died 120 years old. No one knows where he was buried to this day, but the Children of Israel mourned his loss for thirty days. Here eight mourners, representing the whole people of Israel, are congregated about the uncovered body stretched out on a pall, and Moses' face is still shining.

136. JOSHUA CROSSING THE RIVER JORDAN; JOSHUA BEFORE JERICHO. Joshua III. 11–17; IV. 5–6; VI. 8–16, 20. Bronze relief from the so-called 'Porta del Paradiso' by Lorenzo Ghiberti on the Baptistery of S. Giovanni, Florence. About 1440 (see Nos. 11, 20, 29, 72, 76, 114).

The achievements of Joshua are presented in the two principal events of his lifetime: in the crossing of the Jordan dryshod and in the taking of Jericho. The dry river bed of Jordan in the centre and in the left foreground the throng of dumb-founded, incredulous Israelites; behind them the priests with the Ark of the Covenant and

Joshua following on behind, a war-hero in full armour, standing upright in his chariot with helmet and commander's staff. On the opposite bank of the river twelve men have each hoisted a stone ('according unto the number of the tribes of Israel') upon their shoulder, in order to set them up as a memorial of the crossing. Then, on top, the fortress of Jericho stretching away over the whole relief panel and the Israelites marching to encircle it; first the seven trumpeters, then the Ark, then Joshua alone, and finally the people. It is obviously the last moment of the seventh day when 'the people shouted with a great shout' and the walls came tumbling down. The towers of the city walls show cracks and one is already on the point of toppling over.

137. THE FALL OF JERICHO. Joshua VI. Full-page illumination by Jean Fouquet from the Antiquités et Guerres des Juifs de Josèphe. Paris, Bibliothèque Nationale. Ms. fr. 247, fol. 89. About 1470–76. (See No. 123.)

Joshua does not march in procession himself, but directs the people as they pass by him. 'The seven priests' with 'seven trumpets of ram's horns before the ark of the Lord' are right in the foreground and the demolition has already begun, a jumbled heap of stones is all that remains of the city walls.

138–140. Episodes from the Story of Joshua. Three sections of the Joshua Rotulus in the Vatican Library, Rome. Cod. Pal. Gr. 431. 10th century.

In this Byzantine manuscript, still in the early scroll form, in which the events unfold from left to right, unconfined by frames as pictures are, the story of Joshua is told in great detail.

138. THE FALL OF JERICHO. Joshua VI.

The priests blowing the trumpets – here they are short horns – precede the ark coming from the left, while in the centre stands Joshua. His troops on the right, spurred on, are closing with the people of Jericho. The city wall has already fallen down. Two of the men storm forward setting the city alight with torches.

139. ACHAN'S TRESPASS AND PUNISHMENT. Joshua VII. 18–26.

Contrary to the words of the Lord that all plunder from Jericho was to belong to Him, Achan had seized 'a goodly Babylonish garment and two hundred shekels of silver and a wedge of gold' (Joshua VII. 21) and the Lord was angry and Joshua sat in judgement upon him. Achan stands on the left, defending himself before Joshua; in the centre he is being dragged away by the hair to the place of execution; on the right he lies with his kinsfolk in a pit and is being stoned to death by all Israel. 'And Joshua said: Why hast thou troubled us? The Lord shall trouble thee this day' (Joshua VII. 25).

140. JOSHUA'S VICTORY OVER THE FIVE AMORITE KINGS. Joshua x. 22–27.

With God's aid Joshua gains a miraculous victory over the Kings of Jerusalem, of Hebron, of Jarmoth, of Lachish, and of Eglon. After the battle he has them brought before him; from the right they are being dragged past fighting men while Joshua is seated in triumph on a magnificent throne in the midst of his victorious army. The five are then laid in fetters before him. 'Joshua said unto the captains of the men of war which went with him: Come near, put your feet upon the necks of these kings' (Joshua x. 24), as a token of their supreme subjection and as a living witness 'for thus shall the Lord do to all his enemies against whom ye fight'.

141. THE SIEGE OF JERICHO. Joshua VI. Mosaic from S. Maria Maggiore; about 432–440 (see No. 128).

In two strips. *Below:* Joshua with a number of his captains stands full face as the Ark of the Covenant, preceded and followed by trumpeters, passes by him. *Above:* (on the left) the fortress of Jericho, and on the right, Jericho besieged by two armies, is falling in ruins.

142. JEPHTHAH MEETING HIS DAUGHTER. Judges XI. 34. Miniature from a German Bible. Munich, Staatsbibliothek. Cgm. 206, fol. 125 verso. Augsburg. 1457 (see No. 130).

Jephthah makes a vow to the Lord before the great battle with the Ammonites. 'Whatsoever comes forth of the doors of my house to meet me, when I return in peace from the children of Ammon, shall surely be the Lord's, and I will offer it up for a burnt offering' (Judges XI. 31). And the first thing that comes to meet him when he returns victorious is his only child, his daughter, who hurries out to greet him 'with timbrels and with dances'. Here the girl is standing before the door of the house playing the fiddle and her father faces her, still in armour, accompanied by several soldiers.

143. JAEL AND SISERA. Judges IV. 17–21. Pen drawing after the Master of Flémalle in the Herzog Anton Ulrich Museum in Brunswick. About 1430.

Sisera, the commander of the king of Canaan, is defeated by Barak and flees on foot into Jael's tent. She takes him in and covers him up; and when he has fallen asleep, took 'a nail of the tent, and took an hammer in her hand, and went softly unto him, and smote the nail into his temples' (Judges IV. 21).

The artist presents the whole scene on the battlefield: in the background fighting is still going on and the 'tent' in which Sisera takes refuge is part of the camp.

144. JAEL AND SISERA. Judges IV. 17–21. English miniature from the Queen Mary Psalter. London, British Museum. Royal 2B VII, fol. 33 (above). Beginning of the 14th century (see No. 93).

In two adjacent scenes: First (on the left) Sisera asks Jael: 'Give me, I pray thee, a little water to drink.' She has taken him by the hand and he is drinking from a shallow vessel. And then (on the right) the attack upon the sleeping man is carried out. Sisera wears a crown, because in the text beneath he is wrongly qualified as 'Roy Sisera'. The woman is described, equally inaccurately, as Dame Delbola (Deborah). But there can be no doubt as to which is the incident depicted.

145. DEBORAH RIDES INTO BATTLE WITH BARAK. Judges IV. 4–10. French miniature from the St. Louis Psalter. Paris, Bibliothèque Nationale. MS. lat. 10525, fol. 47. About 1252–70.

The prophetess summons Barak and tries to rouse him to do battle with Sisera, but he will only go if she accompanies him. Therefore she rides against the enemy, the only woman among all the heavily armed soldiers.

146. SAMSON SETTING THE FIELDS ON FIRE WITH THE FOXES. Judges XV. 3–5 (see No. 145 – a miniature from the same manuscript). Fol. 58.

Samson, enraged at the insult done to him by the Philistines through his wife, catches 'three hundred foxes, and took firebrands and turned tail to tail, and put a firebrand in the midst between two tails. And when he had set the brands on fire, he let them go into the standing corn of Philistines' and by starting this disastrous fire avenged himself on the Philistines.

147. SAMSON SLAYING A THOUSAND PHILISTINES WITH THE JAWBONE OF AN ASS. Judges XV. 15–16. Floor mosaic in black and white marble in the Cathedral of Siena by Paolo di Martino. 1426.

Samson was bound and handed over to the Philistines but 'the spirit of the Lord came mightily upon him, and the cords that were upon his arms became as flax that was burnt with fire . . . And he found a new jawbone of an ass, and put forth his hand and took it, and slew a thousand men therewith'. In splendid armour and helmet, his hand is raised high to aim a fresh blow; others he has already felled lie piled around him; one is just falling at his feet and the rest of the Philistines are fleeing away on the right.

148. MANOAH'S SACRIFICE. Judges XIII. 20. Painting by Rembrandt in the Staatliche Gemäldegalerie, Dresden. Signed and dated 1641.

'. . . when the flame went up toward heaven from off the altar' (Judges XIII. 20) – this is the moment Rembrandt has illustrated, but in the fullest sense the picture refers to the whole of chapter 13. It is an Annunciation scene; like Sarah, the barren wife of Manoah is promised a son, Samson, the promise being given by a 'man'. At the

RUTH AND BOAZ WITH THE REAPERS.
Woodcut by Hans Holbein.

request of Manoah the 'man' appears once more and repeats the tidings; whereupon Manoah 'took a kid with a meat offering and offered it upon a rock unto the Lord' (Judges XIII. 19). This explains why the angel is portrayed as a 'man' without wings, why the scene takes place out of doors, and why the sacrificial beasts are being burned on a small wood fire on the ground.

149. SAMSON'S WEDDING. Judges XIV. 10–14. Painting by Rembrandt in the Gemäldegalerie, Dresden. Signed and dated 1638.
At the banquet celebrating the marriage of Samson to one of the daughters of the Philistines in Timrath 'they brought thirty companions to be with him. And Samson said unto them: I will now put forth a riddle unto you' (Judges XIV. 11–12). Samson, with thick dark locks, turns away from the bride enthroned behind a magnificent épergne towards the 'companions' and sets his riddle of the lion, gesticulating vigorously with his fingers.

150. SAMSON THREATENING HIS FATHER-IN-LAW. Judges XV. 1–2. Painting by Rembrandt in the Kaiser Friedrich Museum, Berlin. Signed and dated 1635.
An episode very seldom depicted. Samson comes 'in the time of the wheat harvest' to visit his wife, but her father will not let him in, because she had been given to one of his companions meanwhile. The old man offers him the younger, more beautiful sister in her stead. Samson's fury as he shakes his clenched fist up at the old man and the old man's anxious conciliatory expression augur no good for the future.

151. SAMSON WRESTLING WITH THE LION. Judges XIV. 5–6. Painting by Rubens in the National Museum, Stockholm. About 1625.
On his way to the land of the Philistines to win a wife, a young lion comes roaring at Samson, and 'he rent him as he would have rent a kid, and he had nothing in his hand'. The movement with which Samson treads on the spine of the animal and at the same time lays hold of the lion's maw and tears it open, is as bold as it is effective.

152. SAMSON AND DELILAH. Judges XVI. 18–19. Painting by Francesco Morone in the Museo Poldi Pezzoli, Milan. About 1510.
This fatal incident, which Van Dyck, for example, depicts with brutal realism (see colour plate facing Pl. 151) is here transformed into an idyll. One cannot imagine what has taken place nor can one foresee what fearful consequences the charming furtive act of this graceful page will have. With great forethought he has even brought a box with him, in which to carry off Samson's locks. It is scarcely conceivable that this elegant figure in red velvet is Samson, the same man who rent the lion in his bare hands, nor would one suspect that he would one day pull down the house upon the Philistines.

153. RUTH FINDS FAVOUR WITH BOAZ. Ruth II. 10–13. Miniature from the Bible of Jean de Papelou, Paris, Bibliothèque de l'Arsenal. Ms. 5059, fol. 120 verso. 1317.
Boaz who has enquired of his servant about the 'damsel', grants Ruth permission to glean in his field. 'Then she fell on her face, and bowed herself to the ground, and said unto him "Why have I found grace in thy eyes?"' (Ruth II. 10). The miniaturist shows nothing but a corner of the cornfield, some of it cut, some uncut, and the two facing one another, she on her knees, and he showing her favour.

154. RUTH LYING AT BOAZ' FEET. Ruth III. 7–9. Miniature from the Admont Bible. Stiftsbibliothek. Cod. I., fol. 107 verso. Now in the Österreichische Staatsbibliothek, Vienna. About 1130–50 (see No. 121).
Ruth's mother-in-law advised her 'Wash thyself therefore and anoint thee, and put thy raiment upon thee... make... thyself known unto the man' (Ruth III. 3). At midnight, Boaz, startled, leaned forward and saw a woman at his feet who said 'I am Ruth, thine handmaiden, spread therefore thy skirt over thine handmaid' (Ruth III. 8–9). Boaz, his shoes by his couch, has taken Ruth's hand and lifts the cover with his other hand.

155. RUTH AND BOAZ WITH THE REAPERS IN THE FIELD. Ruth II. French full-page miniature from an Old Testament in the Pierpont Morgan Library, New York. MS. 638, fol. 17 verso. About 1250.
Four scenes. *Above left:* Boaz on horseback enquires of his servant about Ruth and, continuing on the right, he directs her to stay with his people and to glean in his fields. *Below left:* Boaz and Ruth share a meal with the

reapers. They sit facing one another, bareheaded, in the shade of a tree 'dipping their morsel into the vinegar' simultaneously (Ruth II. 14). To the right a huge corn-rick which Boaz' labourers are setting up as a sign of his wealth.

156. DAVID THE SHEPHERD; DAVID WRESTLING WITH THE LION; DAVID ANOINTED KING BY SAMUEL. I Samuel XVI. 11 and XVII. 34–35 and XVI. 12–13. Full-page illumination from the Winchester Psalter. London, British Museum. Nero C. IV, fol. 7. Winchester School. About 1150–60.
Above: The Young David as a shepherd in the field; two goats are fighting one another: to the right David wrests the sheep from the lion (I Samuel XVII. 34–35).
Below: David, the youngest and smallest of the brothers, whom the Lord has chosen as king, is anointed by Samuel. His father Jesse and his six brothers look on.

157. DAVID ANOINTED KING BY SAMUEL. I Samuel XVI. 13. Full-page illumination from a Greek Psalter. Paris, Bibliothèque Nationale. Ms. Gr. 139, fol. 3 verso. 10th century. (See No. 174 and colour plate facing pl. 168.)
The scene is played out against a sumptuous classical background with an open colonnade. The aged Samuel pours the oil from a horn over David who stretches out his hands in veneration; the brothers, who have been passed over, and his father Jesse stand by him. A haloed female figure pointing towards him is, like the Naiad in the Vienna Genesis (see Nos. 51, 52), a personification, in this case of 'Magnanimity', the virtue that typified David above all else.

158. DAVID AND GOLIATH. I Samuel XVII. 50–52; XVIII. 7. Bronze relief by Lorenzo Ghiberti on the so-called 'Porta del Paradiso' in the S. Giovanni Baptistery, Florence. About 1440 (see Nos. 11, 20, 29, 72, 76, 114, 136).
The two armies, the Philistines and Israelites, face each other, 'the Philistines stood on a mountain on the one side, and Israel stood on a mountain on the other side; and there was a valley between them' (I Samuel XVII. 3) and they camped in a copse of oak trees, which can all be discerned in Ghiberti's relief. On the left stand the Israelites with Saul in a chariot at their head, while the Philistines on the right, after Goliath has been overthrown, have started to flee in a rout. David is about to cut off Goliath's head with the giant's own sword. In the corner of the foreground is the brook from which David chose 'five smooth stones' (I Samuel XVII. 40). On the horizon beyond the mountains lies Jerusalem, and 'David took the head of Goliath and brought it to Jerusalem' (I Samuel XVII. 54). He can be seen in the middle under the trees, and 'the women came out of all cities of Israel,

singing and dancing. . . . And the women answered one another as they played, and said, Saul has slain his thousands, and David his ten thousands' (I Samuel XVII. 40).

159. DAVID ANOINTED KING BY SAMUEL. I Samuel XVI. 2–13. Byzantine silver bowl from Cyprus in the Metropolitan Museum, New York. 7th century. One of eleven silver bowls, nine of which are decorated with scenes from the life of David.
A strictly symmetrical composition, accentuated by the arch resting on four pillars. In the very centre stands the young David, with Samuel just emptying the anointing horn over his head. Behind David stands his father Jesse, in an attitude of benediction; the two furthest figures are two of David's brothers. Directly beneath is an altar, on which burns the sacrificial flame, with two animals, a ram and a bull, by the side.

160. DAVID AND GOLIATH. I Samuel XVII. 32–40, 49–51, and 54. Intarsia design by Lorenzo Lotto, carried out by Gian Francesco Capodiferro, his son Zanino and his brother Pietro, for the choir-stalls of S. Maria Maggiore, Bergamo. Between 1524–30.
Large in the foreground, a moment seldom chosen: the stone from David's sling strikes the giant's forehead; he staggers under the blow. On the left he lies on the ground and David, with a wide-flung gesture, is about to sever his head from his body. Behind, on a woody hill at the far left, David is to be seen as a shepherd; the bear and the lion, overcome, have taken to flight. On the far right he makes for Jerusalem, holding the severed head, and women, dancing, hasten to meet him. The most astounding part of the composition is the centre where a view of the palace is given, open like a stage; Saul is seated on his throne under a baldaquin and David stands before him, asking permission to go out and save Israel (I Samuel XVII. 32–38).

161. DAVID PLAYING THE HARP BEFORE SAUL. I Samuel XVI. 23 and XVIII. 10–12. Painting by Rembrandt in the Mauritshuis in The Hague. About 1657.
Saul is incensed against David because after the victory over Goliath the women acclaimed him and sang his praises, saying 'Saul hath slain his thousands, and David his ten thousands'. From that day on Saul viewed David with a jaundiced eye (I Samuel XVIII. 9). But when the evil spirit was upon Saul, David played before him on the strings of his harp; Saul holds his javelin in his hand, ready to hurl it. The famous gesture with which Saul draws the curtain across his face in this picture does not mean that he wants to hide his tears but rather his anger and the evil spirit which drives him to throw the spear at David.

162. DAVID PLAYING THE HARP BEFORE SAUL. 1 Samuel XVIII. 10–12. Etching by Lucas van Leyden. About 1509.

The king, possessed of an evil spirit, sits brooding, which is clear from his stooping posture, his clenched hands and the stamping foot. He holds the spear in his hand directed towards David. David, huge and awkward, stands before him unawares and plays on his beautifully curved harp.

163. SAUL AND THE WITCH OF ENDOR. 1 Samuel XXVIII. 11–20. Painting by Salvator Rosa in the Louvre, Paris. 1668.

Saul, when the Lord no longer answered him, 'neither by dreams, nor by Urim nor by prophets' goes to seek advice from one of the witches he had driven out of the land. With two companions he sets out in disguise and asks for the spirit of the newly deceased Samuel to appear in order to receive from him the counsel which the Lord denies him. The man in the white shroud is Samuel who can prophesy only death and destruction for Saul. Saul lies before him on the ground; behind Samuel crouch the two companions. The witch of Endor, a half-naked crone with unkempt hair, works her magic with wand and incense over a tripod; a skeleton, an owl and an animal's skull behind her go to make up the witch's den.

164. DAVID. 1 Samuel XVII. Bronze statue by Dona-tello in the Museo Nazionale, Florence. About 1430–32.

This statue was originally a fountain figure in the court-yard of a Medici palace; David treads the helmeted head of the enemy underfoot, clothed only in greaves, sandals and a shepherd's hat wound with a wreath of leaves. There is nothing arrogant or triumphant in his pose, only relaxed lassitude after a task successfully performed. Of this David it could truly be claimed that he 'was ruddy, and withal of beautiful countenance, and goodly to look to' (1 Samuel XVI. 12).

165. DAVID. 1 Samuel XVII. Marble statue by Michel-angelo in the Accademia, Florence. About 1501–4.

This is David, the victor, at no particular moment in his life: he carries the sling over his shoulder and a stone in his right hand; whether he is taking aim at Goliath or has already done the deed is of no importance. This is David, an image of youthful strength and courage.

166. DAVID WITH THE HEAD OF GOLIATH. 1 Samuel XVII. 54. Painting by Caravaggio in the Galleria Borghese, Rome. About 1605–6.

The moment after he has done the deed: David, with all the gravity of youth, has still his sword in one hand and carries the bleeding head of Goliath by the hair in the other. An old tradition maintains that the head of Goliath is a self-portrait of the painter, Caravaggio, and that his son served as a model for the young David.

167. DAVID WITH THE HEAD OF GOLIATH. 1 Samuel XVII. 54. Painting by Girolamo Forabosco in the Liechtenstein Gallery, Vaduz. About 1665.

David's coat is of tiger skin: he has tucked the sling loosely into his girdle and with the familiar, age-old gesture of the shepherd bringing home the lamb on his shoulder, he has hoisted the burden of the giant head of Goliath on to his.

168. THE DEATH OF SAUL AND HIS SONS. 1 Samuel XXXI. 1–4. Miniature from the Lambeth Bible. Lambeth Palace Library, London. Ms. 3, fol. 151. Canter-bury. About 1150.

The scene of Saul's suicide is seldom represented. The Philistines are routing the Israelites, harassing Saul and killing his sons. The three figures stretched out in the foreground are Jonathan, Abinadab and Melchi-shua, already dead. And the wounded Saul, after his armour-bearer had refused to do it for him, runs himself through with his sword.

169. DAVID MOURNING FOR SAUL AND JONATHAN. 2 Samuel I. 10–12. French miniature by Jean Fouquet from the Antiquités et Guerres des Juifs de Josèphe. Paris, Bibliothèque Nationale, Ms. Fr. 247, fol. 135 verso. About 1470–6. (See Nos. 123, 137.)

The news of the downfall and death of Saul and Jonathan is brought to David by the one man who escaped. The man reports: 'So I stood upon him . . . and I took the crown that was upon his head, and the bracelet that was upon his arm, and have brought them hither unto my lord' (2 Samuel I. 10), and hands him these objects as he kneels. Thereupon David rends his clothes 'and mourned and wept, and fasted until even, for Saul, and for Jona-than his son' (2 Samuel I. 12).

170. THE RECONCILIATION OF DAVID AND ABSALOM. 2 Samuel XIV. 33. Painting by Rembrandt in the Hermitage, Leningrad. Signed and dated 1642.

In order to avenge his sister's shame, Absalom kills his brother Amnon and thus angers his father David, so that he was sent into exile for three years; then he was allowed to return to Jerusalem, but could not look upon the king's face for a further two years, until he was finally forgiven, 'and the king kissed Absalom' (2 Samuel XIV. 32). This is the moment, after years of estrangement, which Rem-brandt has chosen. Before Jerusalem, outlined against the sky, the king receives his son who has come to seek for-giveness. The fact that 'in all Israel there was none to be so much praised as Absalom for his beauty: from the sole of his feet even to the crown of his head there was no blemish in him' (2 Samuel XIV. 25) can be readily believed from this back view of Absalom.

ABSALOM KILLING HIS BROTHER AMNON.
Woodcut by Tobias Stimmer, 1576.

171. KING DAVID. 2 Samuel. Detail from a more than life-size statue by Claus Sluter in the Charterhouse at Champmol, near Dijon. About 1400–1
One of the six Old Testament figures (see Nos. 192, 193, 195) standing on the six-cornered base of what was once a cross of Calvary (the others are: Moses, Jeremiah, Isaiah, Zechariah and Daniel): David is presented as King with his crown, but at what point in his life it is difficult to say; at any rate an experienced man and a sage. The rich border of his mantle adorned with recurring harps proves that Sluter had not only the king in mind but also the psalmist.

172. DAVID THE PSALMIST. 2 Samuel XXII. and Psalms. English miniature from the Rutland Psalter, Belvoir Castle, fol. 97 verso. About 1250.
David the Psalmist is in this case not playing the harp as he usually does, but the organ. A youth treads the bellows for him and another accompanies him on the hurdy-gurdy.

173. ABSALOM CAUGHT IN THE OAK-TREE. 2 Samuel XVIII. 9. French miniature from the Bible Moralisée in the Cathedral Library in Toledo, fol. 126. About 1250 (see Nos. 131, 132).
One of the eight rounds decorating each page of this Bible. The struggle in the wood of Ephraim between the people of Israel and the servants of David is decided in favour of David and 'Absalom met the servants of David. And Absolom rode upon a mule and the mule went under the thick boughs of a great oak; and his head caught hold of the oak, and he was taken up between the heaven and the earth' (2 Samuel XVIII. 9). It should be remembered, too, that 'His hair was so heavy that each year it had to be shorn' (2 Samuel XIV. 26), 'he weighed the hair of his head at two hundred shekels after the king's weight'. Here it has wound itself in single strands around every branch of the tree – Absalom's mule jumps right out of the picture.

174. DAVID AND NATHAN. DAVID'S PENANCE. 2 Samuel XII. Full-page illumination from a Greek Psalter, Paris, Bibliothèque Nationale, Ms. Gr. 139, fol. 136 verso. 10th century (see No. 157 and colour plate facing No. 168).
King David sits on a throne on the left and before him stands Nathan, preaching repentance, reproaching him with his adultery with Bathsheba and the blood of Uriah. In the right foreground David again, on his knees, bent low, imploring the Lord's forgiveness; the woman behind him 'Metonia', the personification of Remorse, props her head in the attitude of Melancholia.

175. BATHSHEBA AT HER TOILET. 2 Samuel XI. 2. Painting by Hans Memling in the Staatsgalerie, Stuttgart. About 1485.
Bathsheba is stepping out of her bath, which is screened off with curtains. She is received by her servant who holds a wrap ready. In the left corner – a small figure – stands David 'upon the roof of the King's house' and sees that 'the woman was very beautiful to look upon'. Water jug and bowl, wooden slippers and a small dog, all help to give the impression of intimacy.

176. BATHSHEBA AT HER TOILET. 2 Samuel XI. 2. Painting by Rembrandt in the Louvre, Paris. Signed and dated 1654.
David is not present, and the letter Bathsheba holds in her hand and her expression implies that this must be a later moment in the story. An old woman is her assistant at the foot-bath.

177. THE JUDGEMENT OF SOLOMON. 1 Kings III. 16–27. Detail of painting by Giorgione, Bankes Collection, Kingston Lacey, Dorset. About 1508.
Solomon, still a young man, sits enthroned, full-face, before a niche (exactly the same arrangement as for a Santa Conversazione), with counsellors close by, two of them young and another old with a white beard. The women are very much akin in age and appearance, both gesticulating, the wicked mother on the left and the true mother on the right.

178. THE JUDGEMENT OF SOLOMON. 1 Kings III. 16–27. Painting by Rubens in the State Museum, Copenhagen. About 1615–17.
Rubens shows the dramatic climax of the dispute, when the king has commanded 'Divide the living child in two, and give half to the one, and half to the other'. The dead child lies on the ground. The executioner has seized the living one brutally by the leg, holding it head downward. He is reaching out to strike. The one kneeling before Solomon is the real mother.

179. THE JUDGEMENT OF SOLOMON. 1 Kings III. 16–27. Ceiling fresco by Raphael in the Stanza della Segnatura, Vatican, Rome. About 1509–11.
This is one of the four rectangles over the corners, two of which are decorated with Old Testament scenes (the other being the Fall of Adam) and two with mythological scenes. Against a gold background in imitation of mosaic, strictly confined to the main figures, the ageing Solomon is seen in profile on his throne, the two women before him. Here, too, the executioner is about to carry out his orders. The woman standing behind Solomon is the real mother.

180. THE EMBARKATION OF THE QUEEN OF SHEBA. 1 Kings x. Painting by Claude Lorrain in the National Gallery, London. Dated 1648.
An episode not expressly mentioned in the Bible. 'The Queen of Sheba heard of the fame of Solomon concerning the name of the Lord' is all that is referred to there. One of Claude Lorrain's most beautiful harbour scenes is enhanced by a procession of small figures descending the steps of the palace on the right, preceded by the regal figure of a woman about to embark. On the quayside and from neighbouring balconies curious bystanders watch the departure.

181. SOLOMON AND THE QUEEN OF SHEBA. 1 Kings x. 1–13. Fresco by Piero della Francesca in the S. Francesco Church, Arezzo. About 1452–9.
With Claude Lorrain the landscape, the atmosphere, the light is everything, the figures are almost an afterthought; with Piero the space is entirely taken up with solid statuesque figures. A panelled wall provides the background to the reception, before which are assembled the Queen and her ladies and the King and his retinue. The Queen bows slightly over the handshake. All wear plain robes, only the King is enveloped in a stiff coat of patterned brocade.

182. SOLOMON AND THE QUEEN OF SHEBA. 1 Kings x. 1–3. The last of the ten bronze reliefs by Lorenzo Ghiberti on the so-called 'Porta del Paradiso' in the Baptistery, S. Giovanni, Florence. About 1440 (see Nos. 11, 20, 29, 72, 76, 114 and 136).
The two meet on the steps of Solomon's temple: the Queen, who has come from Arabia because 'she has heard rumours of Solomon and of the Lord and wants to test him with riddles'; and Solomon, who asked of the Lord, as the supreme favour, 'an obedient heart, so that he may distinguish right from wrong'. Judging from their appearance and their retinue, they are of equal rank; this is underlined by the strictly central composition; they meet each other exactly in the centre before the entrance to the choir.

A LAVER FROM SOLOMON'S TEMPLE.
Woodcut by Tobias Stimmer, 1576.

183. THE TEMPLE OF SOLOMON. 1 Kings v–vi. French miniature by Jean Fouquet from the Antiquités et Guerres des Juifs de Josèphe, Paris, Bibliothèque Nationale. Ms. fr. 247, fol. 163. About 1470–6 (see Nos. 123, 137, 169).
The House, which his father David had not been able to build for the Lord, because he had to wage too many wars, is now being erected by Solomon 'with cedars and stones from Lebanon'. Here the building is far advanced, but not a sign of cedar-wood – it is entirely of stone, a typical French Cathedral in fact, with three portals, all adorned with sculptures. King Solomon, with the architect by his side, stands on a balcony of the adjacent palace, personally directing the building operations.

184. THE DEFEAT OF SENNACHERIB. 2 Kings XIX. 35. Painting by Rubens in the Alte Pinakothek, Munich. About 1616.
Sennacherib, the King of Assyria, bore down upon Jerusalem and threatened to take it, and did 'reproach the living God'. Hezekiah, the king of Judah, prayed for deliverance and through the mouth of Isaiah this was vouchsafed. And it came about, as Isaiah had prophesied; '. . . that night. . . . An angel of the Lord went out, and smote in the camp of the Assyrians an hundred fourscore and five thousand'. A host of angels swoops down from heaven in a halo of light bent on destruction. Everyone beneath falls back in panic: men, horses and standards are struck down in turmoil.

185. KING REHOBOAM. 1 Kings XII. 10. Fragment of a fresco by Hans Holbein the Younger painted for the Grossratssaal, Basle, now Oeffentliche Kunstsammlung, Basle. About 1524–6.
Rehoboam, the son of Solomon, became king and is advised by the elders, how he may lighten the yoke. But not satisfied he seeks the advice of the young men with whom he has grown up, who recommend just the oppo-

site. He should say to the people 'My little finger shall be thicker than my father's loins'. And in Holbein's fresco he accompanies the saying with the appropriate gesture, showing his little finger to the people in illustration.

186. THE PROPHET ISAIAH. Fresco by Raphael in the Church of Sant'Agostino, Rome. About 1512.
This is an isolated figure, on the third pillar of the nave of the church, seated, with two putti in attendance (showing the influence of Michelangelo's frescoes in the Sistine Chapel). Above their heads the putti hold a tablet with a dedication in Greek to Saint Anne, the Madonna and Christ. The prophet exhibits a scroll with a Hebrew inscription of 'Open ye the gates, that the righteous nation which keepeth the truth may enter in' (Isaiah XXVI. 2).

187. JEREMIAH. Fresco by Michelangelo on the ceiling of the Sistine Chapel, Vatican, Rome. About 1511.
One of the seven prophets which, alternating with sybils, flank the scenes of the creation (see Nos. 6–9, 25 and 125). The prophet, meditating with his right hand before his mouth and the left hanging heavy in his lap, grieves over the Jewish people. The two women behind him – the one on the right in mourning clothes and the one on the left turning away in sorrow – are probably the personifications of Israel and Judah, whom the prophet describes as two sisters, who have done evil (Jeremiah III. 6 and 21).

188. THE ASCENSION OF ELIJAH. 2 Kings II. 9–11. Painting by Francesco Polazzo. Samuel H. Kress Collection. Washington, National Gallery of Art. About 1730.
'. . . The Lord would take up Elijah into heaven by a whirlwind' (2 Kings II. 1) and his disciple asks to be allowed to witness it. After the prophet has tried three times to withdraw from him, Elishah's wish is granted, that he may be privileged to see Elijah carried up to heaven in a 'chariot of fire, and horses of fire'. There is scarcely any difference in age between the two figures here, between Elijah, who is carried off in the whirlwind and Elisha, who kneels in adoration on the ground.

189. THE PROPHET ELISHAH AND THE WOMAN OF SHUNAM. 2 Kings IV. 20–30. Painting by Gerbrandt van den Eeckhout in the Museum of Fine Arts, Budapest. Signed and dated 1664.
The prophet had promised the woman of Shunam a son, in gratitude for her repeated hospitality, and the prophecy had been fulfilled; but the son died while still a growing boy. The woman orders an ass to be saddled and sets off to seek the help of Elishah on Mount Carmel. Elishah first sends his servant Gehazi, but he can achieve nothing, and the woman will not leave the prophet until he himself goes and brings the boy back to life.

190. THE CALLING OF JEREMIAH. Jeremiah I. 4–9. Detail of an English miniature from the Winchester Bible, fol. 148 verso. Winchester Cathedral. About 1140.
In the initial letter of the book of Jeremiah, the prophet is shown receiving his call; he hears the word of the Lord but demurs and says 'Ah, Lord God! behold, I cannot speak: for I am a child'. (The banderol is inscribed with the words 'ecce nescio loqui quia puer ego sum' from the Vulgate translation of the text.) But the Lord stooped out of the clouds and 'put forth his hand and touched my mouth. And the Lord said unto me, Behold, I have put my words into your mouth' (Jeremiah I. 9). (These are the very words from the Vulgate on God's banderol: ecce dedi verba mea in ore tuo.) The background is filled with vine shoots which follow the contours of the two animated figures and intertwine around the banderols.

191. ISAIAH. Over-life-size figure in stone in the portal of the abbey church of Souillac (France). About 1140.
One of the two prophets flanking the doorway (the sculptures are no longer in their original position nor in their original arrangement). The prophet Isaiah with banderol and crossed legs and narrow close-fitting garment looks like a brother of the Jeremiah in the English miniature. The same breath of inspiration seems to fill both.

192, 193, 195 (see also No. 171). Three prophets from the so-called Moses Fountain in the Charterhouse at Champmol near Dijon, by Claus Sluter; erected between 1395–1402. They stand, along with David, around the six-cornered base of what was once a cross of Calvary.

192. JEREMIAH. More than life-size statue in stone: the prophet seems to be stepping out of his niche and reading aloud from an open book. He is wearing a turban-like headgear and around his half-closed eyes are fine lines of sorrow.

193. ISAIAH. Over life size statue in stone; a bald head with beautiful long beard, he carries a closed book under his arms and seems lost in contemplation.

194. MICAH. Detail from the Ghent altar by Jan van Eyck. St. Bavo, Ghent. Completed 1432.
The centre panel of this most famous, many-figured altar shows the Adoration of the Lamb. The closed wings represent – besides the portraits of the donors and St. John the Evangelist and St. John the Baptist – the Annunciation to the Virgin, as the beginning of the Story of Redemption. Above Mary, as the instigator, or rather the foreteller of this event, the prophet Micah, a half-length figure, is looking down on the Virgin. His

words of prophecy are written on a beautifully curved scroll above his head: 'Ex te egredietur qui sit dominator in israel', 'out of thee shall come forth unto me that is to be ruler in Israel' (Micah v. 2). As a face of individual stamp it bears a strange resemblance to the Zechariah by Sluter which ante-dates it by thirty years.

195. ZECHARIAH. (See Nos. 193, 194.) Over life-size statue in stone; a sage well versed in the ways of the world, who sees into the hearts of men and looks far ahead into the future.

196. THE ASCENSION OF ELIJAH. 2 Kings II. 9–11. Relief of cedar wood on the door of the Church of S. Sabina, Rome. About 430 (see No. 74).
The steps in the foreground leading up a slight bank are to be taken as an indication of the crossing of the Jordan dryshod. Elijah ascends precipitously in a chariot with two horses who bear him off towards the right 'by a whirlwind', guided by a huge Nike-like angel who floats above him with beautiful outstretched wings.

197. JOB PLAGUED BY THE DEVIL, WITH HIS WIFE AND FRIENDS COMMISERAT-ING. Job II. 7–9 and 11–12. Stone relief from the tympanum of the right door of the North portal of the Cathedral of Chartres. About 1230.
The right door is decorated with figures and scenes from the Old Testament. Job, who is smitten with 'sore boils from the sole of his feet unto his crown . . . took him a potsherd to scrape himself withal; and he sat down among the ashes'. Job is half lying on ashes with a shard in his right hand. The Devil, a skeletal creature, touches him on the head and looks in triumph towards the friends. The wife behind Job puts both her hands to her mouth in horror. Job's comforters, in this case two men and two women, stand around in attitudes of distress.

198. JOB MOCKED BY HIS WIFE. Job II. 9 and 11, 12. Miniature from the Admont Bible, Stiftsbibliothek, Cod. I., fol. 255 verso, formerly at Admont, now in the Vienna Staatsbibliothek. Between 1130–50. (See Nos. 80, 121, 154.)
Job, a bearded man with bald head, lies 'among the ashes', covered from head to foot with boils and turns his face from those around him. His wife stands directly behind him and seems to be saying: 'Dost thou still retain thine integrity? curse God, and die' (Job II. 9). The two men and a woman who 'sat . . . with him upon the ground seven days and seven nights' (Job II. 13) are the friends come to comfort him.

199. JOB AND HIS WIFE. Job II. 9. Painting by Dürer in the Städelsches Kunstinstitut, Frankfurt a.M. About 1503–4.

With the contents of a bucket, the wife drenches the man, who sits wrapt in contemplation. But it is not apparent whether she does this in scorn of Job's faith, steadfast in the face of adversity, or rather to relieve his bodily afflictions. He sits 'upon the ground seven days and seven nights' and speaks not a word (Job II. 13). The fact that he has laid his hands over his mouth is perhaps an allusion to Job XL. 4–5: 'Behold I am vile, what shall I answer thee? I will lay mine hand upon my mouth. Once have I spoken; but I will not answer.'

200. JOB AND HIS COMFORTERS. Job II. 11–13; III, and IV ff. Painting by Luca Giordano in the Escorial, Madrid. About 1695.
Separated from the others by a fence, Job sits 'among the ashes' with his shard, and the three friends Eliphaz, Bildad and Zophar try to console him. Women in the background turn from the painful scene with arms up-raised in distress.

201. THE DESTRUCTION OF THE CHILD-REN OF JOB. Job I. 18–19. Painting by Bernaert van Orley, centre-piece of a Job-altar in the Museum of Brussels. Signed and dated 1521.
A scene not often illustrated: the beginning of the trials of Job. On the same day that his cattle are destroyed his children too are slain. 'There came a great wind from the wilderness; and smote the four corners of the house, and it fell upon the young men, and they are dead.' In an open Renaissance hall, where the children are eating and drinking in the house of the first-born, a wind is blowing in, and a dark thunder-cloud fills the curve of the upper part of the picture. So that we are left in no doubt as to whose handiwork it is, several devils are concealed in the baneful cloud.

202. THE STORY OF JOB. Job II. 1–10 and XXI. 7–12. Painting, right wing of a four-winged altar by the so-called Master of the Legend of St. Barbara in the Wallraf-Richartz Museum, Cologne. About 1480–3.
The story of Job is told in its entirety on two wings of this altar. This is the second wing. After the flocks and children of Job have been destroyed at the instigation of Satan, without Job turning from the Lord, Satan comes to God again, in the left-hand corner, and asks his per-mission to inflict some ailment upon Job, to 'touch his bone and his flesh' (Job II. 4–5). On the right in the middle distance sits Job among the ashes and his wife is scolding him 'Dost thou still retain thine integrity? Curse God, and die'. But Job chides her and says: 'Thou speakest as one of the foolish women speaketh. What? Shall we receive good at the hand of God, and shall we not receive evil?' (Job II. 9–10). In the left foreground he is sitting naked, beaten by the Devil with a 'rod', an obvious allusion to Job's plea: 'Let him take his rod away from me and let not his fear terrify me' (Job IX. 34).

The boils on his body are very clearly discernible. To the right, three wicked men mock Job with music (Job XXI. 12–13), perhaps a confusion with the three friends who came to comfort him. Then in the background, Job and his manifold blessings, after successive tribulations; in the middle room of the house his second family of 'seven sons and three daughters' which the Lord gave him; in front are his recently acquired herds: camels, goats, pigs and fowls, as a sign of the riches that he has won back. On the left an angel clothes him. On the right he lies on his death-bed attended by his wife; angels bear his soul up to God.

203. THE STORY OF JONAH.

Early Christian sarcophagus in the Lateran Museum, Rome. Second half of the 3rd century.

The story of Jonah takes up most of the space on this sarcophagus, while above and between there are other scenes (shown on a smaller scale). The Jonah story begins on the left below with his finding a ship 'going to Tarshish; so he paid the fare thereof and went down into it' (Jonah I. 3). It is a beautiful ship with an enormous sail tossing on the stormy waters. Three mariners are about to throw the naked Jonah overboard, as he had commanded them to do. Right in front of it lies the 'great fish' which the Lord had prepared to swallow up Jonah, a wonderful coiling sea-monster with fangs in his jaws and huge ears, and a tail ending in a crescent moon. Close by lies this same monster – turned towards the right – the coiled tails actually touching each other! – in the act of spewing up Jonah. Above this on the right Jonah stretched out under the gourd (Jonah IV. 5–6) which the Lord made to grow in one night and then wither away again in a night, in order to show Jonah his injustice towards Niniveh. – [Other scenes on the relief: left, above: Christ raising Lazarus; on the right of the great sail: Moses bringing forth water from the rock; on the right of the huge fishes tail: Noah in his Ark.]

204–205. JONAH BEING SWALLOWED BY THE WHALE AND VOMITED UP AGAIN.

Jonah I. 15 and II. 1–11. Two ivory reliefs from the Lipsanoteca, Brescia (see Nos. 87–89), once in S. Giulia, now in the Museo Civico Cristiano, Brescia. About 310–20.

204. The ship, a small cargo boat, whose mast and sails are struck because of the storm, is manned by a crew of six. They are about to throw the seventh, Jonah, overboard into the wolfish open jaws of the sea monster.

205. The monster in all its immensity is just disgorging its three-day visitor.

206. DANIEL IN THE LION'S DEN.

Daniel VI. 16 ff. Ivory relief from the Lipsanoteca in Brescia (see Nos. 87–89, 204–205). About 310–20.

A symmetrical composition, Daniel, naked, in the attitude of an 'orant' (that is with arms raised in adoration), among the lions who sit up quietly like heraldic beasts.

207–208. SUSANNA AND THE ELDERS; SUSANNA BEFORE DANIEL.

Apocryphal Book of the story of Susanna and Daniel I. 16–24 and 50 ff. Ivory relief from the Lipsanoteca in Brescia, formerly in S. Giulia, now in the Museo Civico, Brescia. About 310–20 (see Nos. 87–89, 204–206).

Above: Susanna in her garden which is signified by two oak trees. She wears an ungirt robe, as she is at home, but a light head shawl because she is in the open air. The two old men approach from the left and right and run towards her with outstretched covetous hands. She has raised her arms in protest in the 'Orans' gesture. *Below:* After Daniel's objection, Susanna is brought forth once more. This time Daniel himself administers justice and by hearing the two men separately, he is able to uncover their false testimony and to set Susanna free. This time, as she is outside her home, Susanna wears a girdle over her dress.

209. DANIEL'S VISION.

Daniel VIII. 1–4 and 15–19. Painting by Rembrandt in the Kaiser Friedrich Museum, Berlin. About 1650.

A vision appears to the prophet which he cannot understand: 'there stood before the river a ram with two horns, . . . I saw the ram pushing westward, and northward, and southward.' Daniel is unable to interpret the dream and a 'man' comes to explain it to him (Daniel VIII. 15 ff.). The manner in which the angel, standing behind Daniel, approaches him, is influenced by the description (Daniel X. 10) 'And behold, a hand touched me, which set me upon my knees and upon the palms of my hands. And he said unto me, O Daniel, a man greatly beloved, understand the words that I speak unto thee, and stand upright. . . .' In the attitude and aspect of a guardian angel he points to the ram on the other side of the gorge.

210. DANIEL IN THE LION'S DEN.

Daniel VI. 17–23. Painting by Rubens, formerly in the Duke of Hamilton Collection. About 1616.

In a rocky gorge, a kind of lion's pit, into which nine lions have been huddled together, there is scarcely room for Daniel among them. He sits with folded hands, his gaze directed upwards, in supplication before the God whom he has served unceasingly. The bones and skeleton head lying in the foreground suggest that the lions were only docile in this one case; and their behaviour was otherwise quite reverse.

211. THE THREE YOUTHS IN THE FIERY FURNACE. Daniel III. 21–23. Fresco in the Catacomb of S. Priscilla, Rome. About 230–240.

The three men Shadrach, Meschach and Abed-nego, who served their God despite the orders of Nebuchednezzar and would not worship golden idols, are being thrown fully-clothed into the oven heated to seven times its normal heat; but the fire cannot touch them. They come out again quite unharmed. Here the three stand with arms stretched up to heaven (Orans gesture). The flames flicker around them; as a symbol of salvation a dove with an olive-branch hovers over them. The three men in the fiery furnace were, like Susanna, a favourite theme in early Christian art, because the faithful identified themselves with these figures. The believer could pray 'Deliver, O Lord, the soul of Thy servant, as Thou hast delivered the three men out of the fiery furnace, out of the hand of the wicked king'.

212. SUSANNA AND THE ELDERS. Apocryphal book of the story of Daniel and Susanna. Fresco in the Catacomb of S. Pietro and Marcellino, Rome. Second half of the 4th century.

The garden in which the two elders waylay Susanna is indicated by two trees; she raises both arms to heaven imploringly (Orans Gesture), calling upon the Lord to witness her innocence, just like the three young men in the fiery furnace (see above). This too links in with a prayer for deliverance: 'Deliver, O Lord, the soul of Thy servant, as Thou hast delivered Susanna from the false accusations.'

213. TOBIT HEALED OF HIS BLINDNESS. Tobit XI. 4–5. Full page miniature drawing by an anonymous English master. University Library, Cambridge, Kk. 4.25, fol. 45 recto. About 1200–25.

The father Tobit, blinded by swallow's dung, is made to see again by an ointment of fishes' gall. Although the young Tobias anoints his eyes with it (Tobit XI. 13–15) the angel Raphael says, in the great recognition scene, that God has sent him to heal Tobit (Tobit XII. 4). And so it is the Archangel himself who here places the ointment, with careful fingers, upon the eyes of the old man Tobit.

214. THE ARCHANGEL DEPARTING FROM TOBIT AND HIS FAMILY. Tobit XII. 15–22. Painting by Rembrandt in the Louvre, Paris. Signed and dated 1637.

The happy reunited family, – the old man healed, the young man married, the debt repaid, – wish to thank the 'companion' who has brought all this about and offer him one half of their possessions. But he now says to them 'I will keep close nothing from you' and makes himself known as the angel Raphael, 'one of the seven holy angels, which present the prayers of the saints, and go in before the glory of the Holy One' (Tobit XII. 18). He urges them to thank God, and to spread the truth abroad and then disappears before their eyes. The old man falls to the ground in adoration, the young man kneels in veneration, the mother drops her stick in the shock of recognition, and the young woman looks up with hands reverently joined together. The little dog that had accompanied them on the journey (Tobit VI. 1) is there barking.

215. TOBIT AND HIS WIFE. Tobit X. 1–7. Painting by Rembrandt formerly in the Cook Collection, Richmond, now in the W. van der Vorm, Sr., Collection, Rotterdam. Signed and dated 1659.

The old couple await anxiously the return of their son, delayed by his marriage. The blind father sits idle by the fireside; the mother spins by the window.

216. TOBIAS AND THE ANGEL. Tobit VI. 1–7. Painting by Adam Elsheimer in the National Gallery, London. Between 1600–10.

Young Tobias, with his 'companion', who has promised to lead him safely to Rages in Media and back again, arrives at the waters of the Tigris, where a huge fish threatens to devour him. But his companion shows him how to catch it. Here they are continuing on their journey. Tobias carries the catch tied on a string; before them an open, wooded landscape.

217. TOBIAS AND THE ANGEL CATCHING THE FISH. Tobit VI. 1–5. Painting by Girolamo Savoldo in the Galleria Borghese, Rome. About 1540.

This shows the actual catch, right at the beginning of the journey. The pair, Tobias and the Angel, come to the waters of the Tigris. A huge fish frightens the youth, but the angel tells him what to do. So here he is pulling the fish out of the water without any trouble at all, looking confidently up at the angel. The animal rolled up in the corner on the right is the little dog who ran at their side (Tobit VI. 1).

218. JUDITH WITH THE HEAD OF HOLO-FERNES. Judith XIII. 10. Painting by Botticelli in the Rijksmuseum, Amsterdam. About 1490.

Judith has just stepped out of the 'tent'; it is early morning. She still clasps the sword in her right hand; in the left she holds the severed head of the enemy, as if exclaiming proudly: 'And the Lord smote him by the hand of a woman' (Judith XIII. 15).

219. JUDITH WITH THE HEAD OF HOLO-FERNES. Judith III. 10–11. Painting by Artemisia Gentileschi, Palazzo Pitti, Florence. Between 1621–6.
Immediately after the deed: it is pitch dark. Judith, in a splendid robe, jewels in her hair and in her ears, the sword still in her grasp, has called her maid Abra, and given the severed head to her. She has put it in the basket held ready for it. Both women turn with a sharp movement of the head, as if they were afraid of being followed.

220. JUDITH WITH THE HEAD OF HOLO-FERNES. Judith XIII. 10–11. Paintings by Rubens in the Herzog Anton Ulrich Museum, Brunswick. About 1616–18.
The only light comes from a candle which the old serving woman Abra holds low in her hand. Judith is just handing her the head of Holofernes which she grips by the hair; the old woman takes hold of it by the chin and is about to drop it into the sack held ready.

221. ESTHER BEFORE AHASUERUS. Esther II. 15–17. Painting, centre part of a cassone painting by Filippino Lippi in the Musée Condé, Chantilly. About 1478.
Under a baldaquin sits the king, who has dismissed his queen and is seeking another. Esther, after she has prepared herself for twelve months in the house of the women, like the other maidens, is brought before him; 'and she obtained grace and favour in his sight'. He sits, a dignified figure surrounded by chamberlains, who, like him, are stirred by the sight of Esther.

222. MORDECAI SITS LAMENTING BEFORE THE GATES OF THE PALACE. Esther IV. 1–2. Painting by Botticelli, side panel of a cassone painting belonging to the same series as No. 221, in the Palazzo Pallavicini, Rome. About 1478.
This picture, which has long been mis-interpreted, is now established without question as an episode from the Book of Esther; in fact it is Mordecai sitting before the palace of Ahasuerus. Mordecai, who had adopted Esther as a child, learning of Haman's plots against the Jews, rends his clothes, puts on sack-cloth and laments before the king's gate, in order to attract the attention of Queen Esther and thus to effect the salvation of his people.

223. ESTHER SWOONING BEFORE KING AHASUERUS. Apocryphal chapters to Esther IV. 5–8. Painting by Tintoretto in the Escorial, Madrid. About 1545.

This is the famous second visit which Esther pays to the king, against the king's orders that no-one may see him, upon pain of death, unless he be called to him. But she will speak for her people, and pays no heed to the command: 'If I perish, I perish' (Esther IV. 16). She adorns herself and goes to him with two of her handmaidens. But then, when she sees the king in all his splendour, and he looks angrily at her, she pales and faints away. Caught by her two maids and gazed at in amazement by the crowd of courtiers, the heart of the king is moved at the sight. He rises and is about to lay his golden sceptre upon her shoulder as a sign of favour, ready to grant her whatever she may ask.

224. THE WRATH OF AHASUERUS. Esther VII. 7. Painting by Jan Steen in the Barber Institute, Birmingham. About 1660.
Esther invites the king and Haman to a banquet: there the king grants her a wish and she asks for her people to be spared. And when the king asks who has presumed to lay such schemes against them, she points to Haman sitting at the banquet as the 'wicked adversary'. 'And the king, arising from the banquet of wine in his wrath went into the palace garden.' With rolling eyes and clenched fist, Ahasuerus has obviously shaken the table as he arose, for table vessels lie broken on the floor and a beautiful platter, with a pea-fowl served up on it, is just sliding from the table-cloth. Haman in a feather hat cringes with hands raised to protect himself. The servants in the doorway draw back in alarm.

225. HAMAN IN DISGRACE. Esther VII. 9. Painting by Rembrandt in the Hermitage, Leningrad. About 1660.
Haman, whose shameful machinations have been revealed by Queen Esther, is led away to suffer the fate which he had prepared for Mordecai.

226. THE TABLES OF THE LAW. Exodus XXXIV. Detail of a painting of Moses by Joos van Gent in the Palazzo Ducale, Urbino. About 1475.
Commissioned and inspired by the remarkable Federico da Montefeltre for his palace in Urbino. This is one of twenty-eight portraits in which sages from antiquity, from the Old and New Testament combine with Church luminaries and poets of modern ages, in a gallery of representative heroes. According to an old tradition, it was Montefeltre who, at the surrender of Volterra in the year 1472, took as his only booty the Great Hebrew Bible which is now kept in the Vatican. Hence it is not surprising that the commandments on these Tables of Moses are listed in Hebrew, which was by no means a common occurrence at this date. In the somewhat later fresco in the Sistine Chapel (see No. 115), for example, they are still set down in fantastic exotic-looking script.

NOTES ON THE COLOUR PLATES

Frontispiece
MOSES WITH THE TABLES OF THE LAW,
on his second return from Mount Sinai. Exodus XXXIV.
29. Painting by Rembrandt in the Kaiser Friedrich
Museum, Berlin. Signed and dated 1659.
Moses comes down from Mount Sinai, holding high
above his head the Tables of the Law which have been
entrusted to him a second time, after forty days and
nights upon the mountain. The contours of the mountain
are just visible behind him; and so he brings to the 'stiff-
necked' people the Commandments of its 'jealous' God.
Rembrandt, without using any exterior attributes such
as halo or horns, makes the skin of Moses' face shine, as
if in reflection of God's glory.

Facing Pl. 12.
THE GARDEN OF EDEN: THE CREATION
OF ADAM AND EVE, THE FALL, THE
EXPULSION. Genesis II. Painting by Lucas Cranach
in the Kunsthistorisches Museum, Vienna. 1530.
A green, open landscape, tree-studded and watered by a
spring: the Garden of Eden, and therein the story of the
first man and woman, in six episodes, beginning, on the
far right, with the creation of Adam from a clod of
earth; God is laying His hand on his head in blessing. At
the water's edge, the creation of Eve from Adam's rib, a
parturition in which God lends an active hand. Big in the
foreground, centre, Adam and Eve, being blessed and
cautioned by God. Behind, near the left border, the
Expulsion; an angel with drawn sword chases the couple
away. The great charm of the picture lies in the many
animals scattered about between these groups, in pairs, as
they are when filing into the Ark, with the exception of
the dog, a greyhound, lying alone at Eve's feet. But
otherwise the animal world is a reflection of the human
pair: in the right foreground, at the very front, a pair of
magnificent horses. On the other side of the thicket
behind which Adam and Eve hide from God, two black
bears. The green garden swarms with pairs of pheasants,
peacocks, storks, swans, harts and roes.

Facing Pl. 36.
LOT AND HIS DAUGHTERS. Genesis XIX.
29–36. Painting by Lucas van Leyden in the Louvre,
Paris. About 1521.
It is the night of the destruction of Sodom and Gomorrah;
the rain of fire falls like shooting stars from heaven upon
the city lying by the water's edge, which is partly going
up in smoke, and partly being engulfed by the sea. In
front of it is a foot-bridge with the easily recognizable
silhouettes of Lot and his two daughters and an ass upon
it; behind them the mother has already turned into the

pillar of salt. Before a tent in the left foreground, Lot
embraces one daughter, while the other fills a pitcher
from a flagon of wine. A torch in an iron stand lightens
the darkness.

Facing Pl. 57.
JACOB WRESTLING WITH THE ANGEL.
Genesis XXXII. 25–30. Painting by Rembrandt in the
Kaiser Friedrich Museum, Berlin. About 1659.
During the night before the reconciliation with Esau a
'man' appeared to Jacob and wrestled with him 'until the
breaking of the day. And when he saw that he prevailed
not against him, he touched the hollow of his thigh; and
the hollow of Jacob's thigh was out of joint' (Genesis
XXXII. 24–25). From then on Jacob bore the name of
Israel. Rembrandt shows the very moment when Jacob's
hip is being wrenched. The hand of the tremendous
powerful angel grips the hip joint, and the angel presses
his knee against Jacob's other side, in order to force the
man before him, who is standing his ground. The
violence of this movement contrasts oddly with the
look of quiet concentration on their faces. Man and angel
look strangely alike, almost reflections of one another,
equal in strength and endurance.

Facing Pl. 95.
MOSES BEFORE THE BURNING BUSH.
Exodus III. 2–6. Painting by Domenico Feti in the
Kunsthistorisches Museum, Vienna. Before 1614.
It is the moment after Moses has received God's summons,
while tending his father-in-law's flocks – one huge animal
is at his side – and he is about to take off the second sandal.
Immediately before him is the Burning Bush, the sign of
the presence of God, although He himself is not visible.

Facing Pl. 151.
SAMSON AND DELILAH. Judges XVI. 18–19.
Painting by Van Dyck in the Dulwich Gallery, London.
Before 1620.
Under repeated pressure, after he has quibbled three
times, Samson has 'told her all his heart', and revealed to
Delilah wherein his strength lies. 'And she made him sleep
upon her knees: and she called for a man, and she caused
him to shave off the seven locks of his head' (Judges XVI.
19). Clad only in an apron of hide, he lies sleeping heavily,
pressed close to her. Two servant women bend over
Delilah's shoulder, full of wanton curiosity to see Samson
being shorn of his black locks by an elderly man with
huge shears. And in the background on the left armed
Philistines are ready, waiting to bind him, to blind him,
and fetter him with iron chains: the brutal outspokenness
of the young Van Dyck is most impressive.

Facing Pl. 160.
THE ANOINTING OF DAVID. 1 Samuel XVI.
1–13. Painting by Paolo Veronese in the Kunsthistorisches Museum, Vienna. About 1564.
The Lord orders Samuel to arise and to anoint the young David. But Samuel feared the wrath of Saul, if he should learn of his intention; therefore God advises him to pretend to be sacrificing a calf. And so the scene here takes place in front of an altar table before a temple wall, in the midst of sacrificial beasts; the left side opens onto ruins, and the right onto a river with bridge and a stately palace. Instead of an animal sacrifice preparations are being made for an event of greater import: the young David kneels with arms crossed on his breast and behind him Samuel is filling the anointing horn, in order to consecrate him as king. The old man on the left with the blue cap is David's father Jesse, with David's six brothers around.

Facing Pl. 168.
DAVID PLAYING THE HARP. 1 Samuel XVI. 18. Byzantine miniature from the Greek Psalter, Paris, Bibliothèque Nationale, Ms. Gr. 139, fol. 1. 10th century. (see Nos. 157, 174).
The young David holds the lyre in his lap and plays amid his flocks of sheep and goats, his sheep-dog next to him. The woman sitting behind him with her arm resting on his shoulder is the personification of 'Melodia'. Behind the garlanded stele on the right the head of a second nymph, probably Echo, and big in the foreground, the urban deity 'Bethlehem'. A bucolic idyll, antique in the composition of the whole as well as in the facial types and in the classic personifications. It is the first illuminated page of a famous psalter and illustrates the beginning of the life story of David.

Facing Pl. 186.
ISAIAH. Ceiling fresco by Michelangelo in the Sistine Chapel in the Vatican, Rome; about 1511 (see Nos. 6–9, 25, 28, 125 and especially No. 187).
In contrast with Jeremiah, an old man, whose whole attention is turned inward, this young Isaiah is startled by the call of the youth behind him. He has closed his book and listens with intense concentration to the voice that rouses him.

Facing Pl. 217.
TOBIAS WITH THE THREE ARCHANGELS. Tobit VI. Painting by Botticini in the Uffizi, Florence. About 1467.
Tobias, proceeding on his journey to Media, has already had his adventure with the great fish; he carries it with him in a sling. His little dog is there too and he is holding the hand of his own special guardian angel, Raphael, who carries as his attribute the box containing the eye-ointment in his right hand. He is flanked by Gabriel on the right, characterized as the Angel of the Annunciation by the lily stem, and by Michael on the left, identified as the slayer of the dragon by his armour and drawn sword. Thus the picture is transformed from an episode in the book of Tobit into a votive picture of the three Archangels.

On page 17.
LOT'S WIFE TURNED TO A PILLAR OF SALT: ABRAHAM AND ISAAC ON THE WAY TO MORIAH. Genesis XIX. 24, 26, 30, and XXII. 3, 5–7. Miniature from the Sarajevo Haggadah, fol. 7 verso, a Spanish-Jewish manuscript of the 14th century (see Nos. 120, 129).
Like all the illustrations in this manuscript there are two scenes, one on top of the other. *Above:* The destruction of Sodom; a cluster of buildings on the right, on which a rain of fire is falling; in the centre (enormous in comparison with the city and the other figures), is Lot's wife turned into a pillar of salt, whose face is still recognizable turned towards the city. Then on the left, Lot, a smaller figure, with his two daughters, here shown as children – whom he urges along before him. *Below:* On the way to the sacrifice; Abraham, dressed in priestly robes with the sacrificial knife and a small bowl in his hands, strides after Isaac, who is about to ascend the mountain, with the bundle of wood on his back. Two servants with an ass remain behind at the foot of the mountain.

NOTE ON THE ILLUSTRATIONS ON PAGES 209, 219, 221, 225, 228, 229:

Holbein's woodcuts to the Old Testament, cut by Hans Lützelburger, were probably finished before 1526, but were first published in 1538 by Trechsel in Lyons. The series consists of 88 Biblical pictures (and four prints to Genesis in a different format, which were taken over from the 'Dance of Death'). The illustrations on pp. 228–9 reproduce woodcuts by Tobias Stimmer, a Swiss mannerist who specialized in portrait woodcuts. His woodcuts to the Bible were first published in 1576 in the "Neue künstliche Figuren Biblischer Historien' published by Gwarin in Basle.

INDEX OF PLACES

THE FINDING OF MOSES. Wall-painting from the Synagogue at Dura-Europos, Syria. 3rd century A.D.

INDEX OF ARTISTS

WORKS BY UNKNOWN ARTISTS